# WILDLIFE
## OF THE
# LOWVELD

### Common Animals and Plants

#### INCLUDING KRUGER NATIONAL PARK

**Duncan Butchart**

## *for Tracey*

## Acknowledgements

Many friends and colleagues have assisted me in the compilation of this book and their support is greatly appreciated. Valuable comments on the introductory sections were provided by Ann Cameron, Bob Scholes and Lex Hes. Individual sections were read by specialists in their fields: John and Sandie Burrows (plants), Vincent Carruthers (frogs), Paul Skelton (fishes) and Buster Culverwell (reptiles); any errors are, however, of my own making. The names of the photographers who supplied material additional to my own are listed alongside their respective pictures. I am particularly grateful to Lex Hes, Chris & Tilde Stuart, Vincent Carruthers, Paul Skelton, Peter Lawson, Colin Bell, Mark Tennant and Beth Peterson for their generous provision of photographs, and to James Marshall for the loan of photographic equipment. Brendan Ryan and John Carlyon kindly permitted the use of photographs at a reduced rate. My exploration of the Lowveld and my understanding of its ecology, animals and plants has been enhanced by Buster Culverwell, while he was based at Mbuluzi Game Reserve in Swaziland, and by James Marshall, while he was based at Londolozi Game Reserve in the Sabi-Sand. I am also thankful to Peter Hancock and Joe Venter, then of Manyeleti Game Reserve, for inviting me to carry out field work in 1980. Thanks also to Conservation Corporation Africa, whose properties – Londolozi, Ngala and Bongani – I have had the privilege to visit and work at in recent years. I am grateful to Southern Book Publishers for initially publishing this title as *Wild About the Lowveld* and to the Natural History team at Struik for this new edition. Finally, I thank my wife Tracey for keeping me on track for the duration of this project, and for her love and encouragement – this book is dedicated to her.

Struik Publishers
(a division of New Holland Publishing (South Africa) (Pty) Ltd)
Cornelis Struik House
80 McKenzie Street
Cape Town, 8001
South Africa
**www.struik.co.za**

First published in 1996 by Southern Book Publishers
Published in 2001 by Struik Publishers

10 9 8 7 6 5 4 3 2 1

Cover photographs: **Front cover:** Top left, Lion (SIL); Top right, Lilacbreasted Roller (Nigel Dennis/SIL); Upper middle right, Barberton Daisy (Duncan Butchart); Lower middle right, Brownbacked Tree Frog (Duncan Butchart); Bottom right, Giraffe (Andrew Bannister/SIL); Bottom left, Hippo (Nigel Dennis/SIL) **Back cover:** Top, Bateleur (Nigel Dennis/SIL); Bottom, Variable Skink (Leonard Hoffman) (SIL = Struik Image Library)

Designed and typeset by Groundhog Graphics, Nelspruit
Reproduced by Hirt & Carter, Cape Town (Pty) Ltd
Printed and bound by NBD, Drukkery Street, Goodwood, Western Cape

ISBN: 1 86872 642 8

By covering a broad spectrum of wildlife species, this book is designed to open the eyes of those interested only in specific groups, such as large carnivores or birds, to a bigger picture in which all living things interact. With the Lowveld's tremendous diversity of animals and plants, the choice of species has been strict with the result that a number of not uncommon species have been excluded. Details of more comprehensive publications are therefore given at the beginning of each group and in the list of references and further reading on p. 122.

Visitors to the KNP or other wildlife reserves of the Lowveld may gain the impression that the future of the animals and plants is secure for all time. But as the 21st Century approaches, these conservation areas face a number of challenges and uncertainties.

Regrettably, but unavoidably, the history of the KNP is caught up in the legacy of the former non-democratic era, and much has to be done for it to gain the full support of surrounding communities. The former 'homelands' of Kangwane, Gazankulu, Lebowa and Venda, which border the KNP, exhibit severe land degradation and resource depletion brought about by large numbers of impoverished, land-hungry people. If the conservation areas are to be saved in the long-term, ways must be found to ensure that these neighbours may derive sufficient economic benefits from tourism and harvesting in order that they can improve their lifestyle without expanding their marginal agricultural activities.

Of equal concern to the conservation of biodiversity and ecological processes within wildlife reserves, and indeed to all the people of the region, is the impact that intensive agriculture and industry is having on the rivers which flow into the Lowveld. In a country where nature-based tourism has the potential to be the greatest employer of people and the highest earner of foreign revenue, concern is growing over the expansion of thirsty timber plantations and other monocultures, such as sugar, which require intensive irrigation and reduce river flow.

Ironically, the increased numbers of tourists visiting the region pose problems regarding the maintenance of the very factors which draw them there: the observation and appreciation of wildlife under natural conditions. In the busy KNP, sensitive management of tourist activity to reduce negative impacts, is a growing priority.

# HOW TO USE THIS GUIDE

## The animals and plants

Most of the life forms which you are likely to see in the region are featured, with an emphasis on mammals, birds and trees – the groups of greatest interest to most visitors. Species are arranged in such a way that those with similar characteristics appear together, even though this sequence may differ from standard reference works. In addition to the species featured, mention is made of less common similar species (marked 'ss') with which they might be confused. Due to limitations of space, invertebrates are not treated in any detail, but it is hoped that the information provided will create some awareness of this fascinating, and often hard to ignore, group of animals. Of the plants, only the larger trees are treated in detail, although some of the more colourful, smaller plants and common grasses are also covered. Alien (non-indigenous) species are marked with an asterisk (*).

The names of all species follow those of the most recent authoritative publications, but in line with ornithological literature – and in order to standardise terminology in this guide – hyphens have been eliminated from all double-barrelled common names. The scientific names of trees and other plants are used ahead of common names, as the latter often differ from region to region, and frequently relate species to families to which they do not belong. The name of the family to which each plant belongs is included for this reason; since they are widely used, the Afrikaans names of plants are provided where known. Scientific terms have been kept to a minimum but could not be completely avoided; an abbreviated glossary of these terms is provided on p. 123.

At the beginning of each section introductory notes provide an overview of the group and recommended reference books are listed. In addition, a detailed list of books for further reading is given on p. 122.

## The habitats

Seven distinctive habitats, from bush savanna to rivers and wetlands, are identified and their characteristics described. Recognition of the habitat that you are in is an important aspect of identification, as many species are specific to certain vegetation or soil types. Colour-coded symbols for each habitat link each species with the habitat/s in which it is most likely to be encountered, but to which it is not necessarily restricted. Man-made habitats are not included, although gardens – whether in towns, around hotels or restcamps – provide suitable habitat for a variety of wildlife, particularly birds.

## The photographs

Where possible, photographs have been selected or taken to best depict key identification features. Where male and female of one species differ, the sex not illustrated is described in the text. It should be remembered that the time of day during which a photograph was taken, and the resultant variation in lighting, may influence the colours of the subject. Some difficult-to-photograph species are illustrated with colour paintings.

In the case of plants, most have been photographed in close-up, to best illustrate leaves, flowers or fruit; but because other features – such as shape, height and bark – are often vital in identification, the text must be closely referred to.

# Northern Lowveld

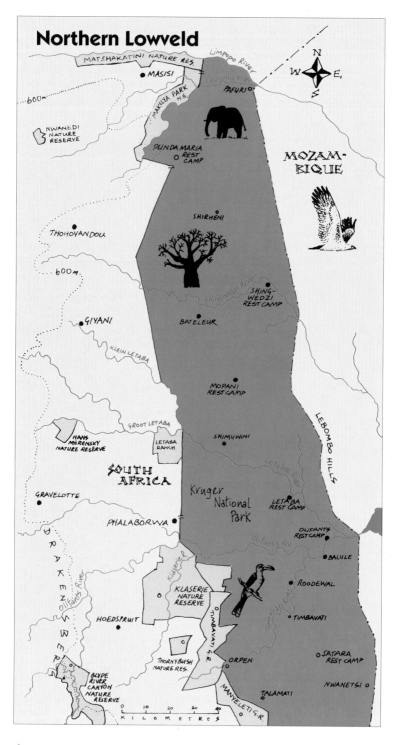

Matshakatini Nature Res.
Limpopo River
MASISI
Makuya Park N.R.
PAFURI
Luvuvhu River
600m
NWANEDI NATURE RESERVE
MOZAM-BIQUE
PUNDA MARIA REST CAMP
SHIRHENI
THOHOYANDOU
600m
SHING-WEDZI REST CAMP
Shingwedzi River
GIYANI
BATELEUR
KLEIN LETABA
MOPANI REST CAMP
GROOT LETABA
HANS MERENSKY NATURE RESERVE
LETABA RANCH
SHIMUWINI
SOUTH AFRICA
Letaba River
LEBOMBO HILLS
GRAVELOTTE
Kruger National Park
LETABA REST CAMP
PHALABORWA
OLIFANTS REST CAMP
Olifants Riv.
DRAKENSBERG
Olifants River
BALULE
Klaserie R.
KLASERIE NATURE RESERVE
ROODEWAL
HOEDSPRUIT
TIMBAVATI S.R.
Timbavati River
TIMBAVATI
THORNYBUSH NATURE RES.
SATARA REST CAMP
BLYDE RIVER CANYON NATURE RESERVE
ORPEN
NWANETSI
MANYELETI S.R.
TALAMATI

0  10  20  30  40
KILOMETRES

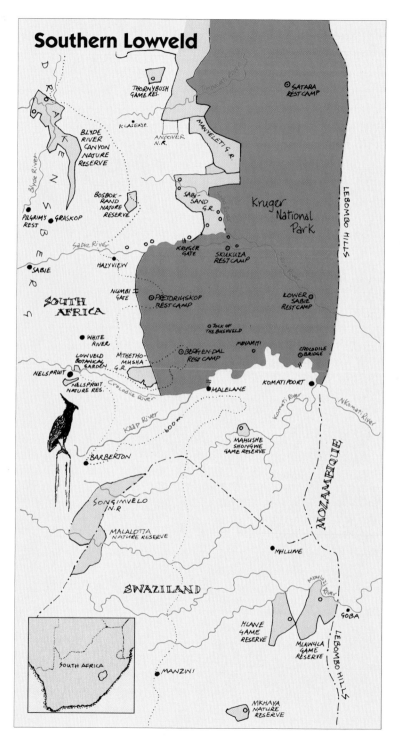

# Southern Lowveld

THORNYBUSH GAME RES.

○ SATARA REST CAMP

BLYDE RIVER CANYON NATURE RESERVE

Timpovati River

K LASERIE

ANDOVER N.R.

MANYELETI G.R.

BOSBOK-RAND NATURE RESERVE

PILGRIM'S REST · GRASKOP

SABI-SAND G.R.

Kruger National Park

LEBOMBO HILLS

Sabie River

SABIE

HAZYVIEW

KRUGER GATE

SKUKUZA REST CAMP

NUMBI GATE

SOUTH AFRICA

○ PRETORIUSKOP REST CAMP

○ JOCK OF THE BUSHVELD

LOWER SABIE REST CAMP

WHITE RIVER

LOWVELD BOTANICAL GARDEN

MTHETHO-MUSHA G.R.

○ BERG-EN-DAL REST CAMP

MBYAMITI

CROCODILE BRIDGE

NELSPRUIT

NELSPRUIT NATURE RES.

Crocodile River

MALELANE

KOMATI POORT

Kaap River

600m

Komati River

NKomati River

MAHUSHE SHONGWE GAME RESERVE

BARBERTON

MOZAMBIQUE

SONGIMVELO N.R

MALALOTJA NATURE RESERVE

MHLUME

SWAZILAND

Mbuluzi River

GOBA

LEBOMBO HILLS

SOUTH AFRICA

HLANE GAME RESERVE

MLAWULA GAME RESERVE

MANZINI

MKHAYA NATURE RESERVE

7

# GEOLOGY AND TOPOGRAPHY

The lie-of-the-land, or topography, is a direct result of the geological history of an area as well as of processes such as erosion and deposition. These processes are often difficult to grasp by the non-specialist, however, and few people show much interest in the rocks around them or the soil beneath their feet. This is unfortunate, as these features reveal the processes responsible for landscape formation.

A simplified overview of the geology of the Lowveld reveals that prior to the breaking up of the huge super-continent of Gondwanaland (South America, Africa, India and Australia were previously joined) about 250 million years ago, the ancient bedrock of **granite** was overlain by sedimentary **ecca shales** during a very wet climatic period. Following this, and in the process of Africa unshackling itself, volcanic activity forced molten lava through the Earth to deposit layers of **basalt** and then **rhyolite** on top of the shale. When Africa finally stood alone, some 135 million years ago, the continent tilted dramatically to the east exposing each of the layers or strata. Subsequent erosion weathered certain rock types more rapidly than others to form the shallow basin we see today between the Drakensberg and Lebombo Hills.

In many places, the Lowveld basin is walled in on its western edge by the steep escarpment of the Drakensberg, but several east-flowing rivers cut through this barrier to create spectacular scenery. Nowhere is this more impressive than at the rugged Blyde River Canyon (pictured below, with the lowveld plains in the distance).

In the west, at the base of the Drakensberg, the undulating countryside is dominated by granite which is exposed in places in the form of domes or outcrops of balancing boulders. This granite is estimated to be over 3 500 million years of age, making it among the oldest rocks on Earth. East of the hilly granite country is a broad, level plain of soils derived from basalt, which eroded rapidly in comparison with the granite. Sandwiched between the layers of granite and basalt is a narrow, discontinuous band of soils derived from ecca shales. To the west of the basalt plains are the Lebombo Hills, consisting of volcanic rhyolite, which intruded above the basalt to stand above the plains.

BETH PETERSON/AFRICAN IMAGES

# CLIMATE

The Lowveld has a sub-tropical climate with hot, wet summers and warm, dry winters. Temperature decreases and rainfall increases with altitude: the foothills, between 1 500 and 600 m, are coolest and wettest while Pafuri (at the junction of the Levuvhu and Limpopo rivers) and Komatipoort (on the Crocodile River), at an altitude of less than 200 m, are driest and hottest.

Rain falls mostly between October and March, usually in the form of short thunderstorms. Higher altitudes experience regular morning mists in summer. Average annual rainfall in the extreme north of the KNP at Pafuri is 375 mm, while Nelspruit and Pretoriuskop have an average of 740 mm. Long-term monitoring suggests that alternating wet and dry (drought) cycles may occur approximately every ten years.

Daytime temperature in summer (November-February) often rises well above 30 °C , dropping to about 18 °C at night. Humidity may be high. In midwinter (June-July) the daily average is 23 °C, sometimes dropping to below 5 °C at night. Frost occurs occasionally along the Crocodile River at Nelspruit, and more often higher up in the foothills.

# IDENTIFYING AND WATCHING WILDLIFE

Due to the occurrence of numerous potentially dangerous large mammals, exploration of the wildlife reserves of the Lowveld is done mostly by vehicle. Walking opportunities are available, however, on the popular KNP walking trails or excursions from private lodges – under the guidance of an experienced guide – and these allow you to see many of the smaller life forms. Although being in a vehicle has its limitations in terms of direct contact with nature, there are advantages as most animals, including birds, are much less concerned about vehicles than they are about people, and often allow a close approach. This is especially true on the well-used tourist routes. Photography is also far easier from a vehicle which acts as a hide and provides a lower vantage point than if you are on foot. Travelling by vehicle is best in the early mornings and late afternoons, when animals are most active. In the dry winter months, parking at a waterhole or pan, and simply waiting, is one of the most rewarding (and relaxing) ways of seeing wildlife.

Birds, and smaller creatures such as bats, reptiles, frogs and insects, are often common around restcamps, picnic sites and the gardens of lodges and hotels, so it is wise to spend time exploring these surroundings. Trees and other plants are also best studied in such places where leaves, bark and flowers can be closely examined.

Outside of the KNP and other reserves, walking opportunities exist at such places as the Blyde River Canyon Nature Reserve and Nelspruit Nature Reserve where the absence of potentially dangerous large mammals allows you to safely stalk and watch birds and other wildlife. Almost all gardens in the Lowveld, whether in towns or around farmsteads, abound with birds and smaller wildlife whose presence can be further encouraged by the planting of indigenous trees and shrubs, and the provision of regular water during the dry winter months.

Before setting out to explore the Lowveld, it is a good idea to make yourself familiar with the species which you are likely to see by studying this book; the habitat symbols alongside the species accounts will guide you to the places where you are most likely to find certain animals and plants. Keeping a diary or notebook of interesting observations and sightings is a good way of building up your knowledge. Notes on the numbers within a herd or group, what they are eating, and any evidence of breeding activity, are worth documenting and greatly enhance a checklist of species recorded. Remember to note the date and time of day, and consider keeping all your nature notes in a journal or file. Don't hesitate to make written notes in your field guides – including this one – as these may be of use later for the rapid identification of the same or similar species.

Consideration for wildlife should always take priority. While in the KNP drive slowly so as not to disturb the animals you hope to see and try not to stop too suddenly. If you are seated in an open vehicle (at a private lodge) avoid sudden movements and speak softly at all times. The now popular activity of the 'night-drive' allows a glimpse into the nocturnal world of wildlife but care should be taken not to unduly disturb or compromise animals being observed under spotlight. Most animals will 'freeze' when illuminated and are therefore at extreme risk to predators that may be on the scene. Put yourself in the position of the animal and avoid beaming the light directly into its eyes. Getting close to a wild animal is a hollow experience if you disrupt its life in the process.

# HABITAT DESCRIPTIONS

Planet Earth can be divided into several broad categories of land type. Geographers refer to these as **vegetation zones**, which include well-known types such as forest and desert. Recognising the interrelatedness of all life forms, ecologists prefer to use the word **biome** for these broad definitions so as to embrace all the components (living and non-living); the Lowveld falls within the **savanna** biome.

A biome is dictated largely by **climate**, but **geology** – which determines topography and soil type, and in turn the **structure of the vegetation** – creates different **habitats**.

With the exception of rocky outcrops, rivers and wetlands, and the narrow strips of evergreen trees which form forests along watercourses, much of the Lowveld may appear fairly uniform in appearance. A closer examination of this landscape – which reveals the characteristics of each habitat – is not only fascinating in itself, but is also a useful means of locating and identifying particular plants and animals. Ecologists may use different habitat classifications for different purposes, but for this book the **height and spacing of woody plants** are the criteria used.

Seven habitats are defined on the following pages and the characteristics of each briefly described; some typical plants and animals are also mentioned. In most cases these habitats rarely divide into neat blocks and a great deal of merging and overlap occurs. In such areas – known as **ecotones** – species diversity is often at its greatest.

The colour-coded symbols at the top of each habitat page are used throughout the species accounts as a means of indicating where particular animals and plants are most likely to be seen.

## Key to habitat symbols

**EF** Escarpment Foothills

**B** Bush Savanna

**T** Tree Savanna

**G** Grass Savanna

**RO** Rocky Outcrops

**RF** Riverine Forest

**RW** Rivers and Wetlands

# Escarpment Foothills

To the west of the Kruger National Park and the Lowveld proper, but below the great wall of the Drakensberg, are the rolling escarpment foothills. Ranging in altitude **from 1 500 to 600 metres above sea level**, they become cooler and wetter the higher you go.

This area is a **mosaic of rocky hillsides, bushland, grassland and forested ravines** which, for the purposes of this book, is considered a single habitat. Although pockets of Afromontane-mistbelt forest exist (notably near Tzaneen, Mariepskop, Sabie and Kaapschehoop), they are not considered here.

Natural habitats are fragmented by the vast plantations of exotic pines and eucalyptus, and orchards of citrus and other commercial fruit trees now blanket the landscape. The pockets of uncultivated land are of interest to naturalists as they support a wide variety of plants and animals uncommon at lower altitudes: Longcrested Eagle, Purplecrested Lourie, Bluegrey Flycatcher, Wood Owl and African Goshawk being examples.

The base of the Blyde River Canyon, contained within the surrounding nature reserve, is the largest and most accessible portion of the natural foothills. The bustling town of Nelspruit is surrounded by attractive granite domes and wooded valleys, a small portion of which is conserved in the Nelspruit Nature Reserve (pictured above). Typical trees here are the Paperbark Thorn *Acacia sieberiana*, Kiaat *Pterocarpus angolensis* and Lowveld Chestnut *Sterculia murex*. Similar landscapes exist around Barberton and Hazyview. Much of the beautiful Schoemanskloof Valley, between Lydenburg and Nelspruit, remains uncultivated and it is hoped that nature-tourism opportunities may soon be developed by the private landowners in this area.

# Bush Savanna

**Bush savanna** – which may also be termed 'bushveld' – is characterised by **the majority of woody plants (trees and shrubs) being less than 6 metres in height** and with **little space between their crowns**. Taller trees often break this low cover. This is the predominant habitat in the Lowveld, occurring primarily on **granite**, **basalt** and **ecca shales**. Topography and soil type influence the plant species which dominate in particular areas. Impala, Kudu and Warthog are common, as are various hornbills, shrikes, francolins and smaller raptors.

In the hilly **granite country** of the western Lowveld, coarse sandy soils, with poor water-holding capabilities and leached of nutrients, occur on the **crests and slopes** where they support a community of deciduous **broadleaved trees**. The Red Bushwillow *Combretum apiculatum*, and other members of this family, prevails. Grasses here are fibrous, but favoured by species such as Sable. In **valley bottoms** the accumulation of nutrient-rich, water-holding clay soils support **fineleaved trees**, most armed with thorns. Scented Thorn *Acacia nilotica* and Sicklebush *Dichrostachys cinerea* are among the most abundant; in the northwest, low Mopane *Colophospermum mopane* takes the place of the fine-leaved trees. Grasses are nutritious. The extensive **basalt flats** in the northeast are dominated by shrubby Mopane, stunted due to an impervious layer of calcrete below the clays, by sodic soils, or due to low rainfall. Grasses here are palatable but sparse. Bird diversity is low.

The narrow band of poorly-drained **ecca shales**, as can be seen between Satara and Crocodile Bridge, tend to be dominated by acacia thickets.

Various species of *Commiphora* dominate the semi-arid region in the far north of the KNP between the Limpopo and Levuvhu rivers.

# Tree Savanna (Woodland)

**Tree savanna**, or woodland, is characterised by trees of **6 metres or more in height with crowns touching, or nearly so**. Scrubby undergrowth and grass is sparse. In the Lowveld, this habitat is limited in the KNP, perhaps due to elephant which push over trees to browse on their foliage, and in the west due to agriculture and settlement. Woodland occurs mostly on sand in the slightly moister areas (above 650 mm).

In the southeast KNP, on the **granite soils** around Pretoriuskop, Silver Terminalia *Terminalia sericea* forms tree savanna on hill slopes where Marula *Sclerocarya birrea* and Kiaat *Pterocarpus angolensis* are also prominent.

The **sandstone-derived soils** near the Punda Maria restcamp in the northern KNP support a tree savanna composed of species absent or rare elsewhere in the region. Pod Mahogany *Afzelia quanzensis* and White Syringa *Kirkia accuminata* being among the larger trees.

The most extensive and impressive tree savanna in the KNP occurs to the east of Punda Maria restcamp on **ecca shales**. Here, tall Mopane *Colophospermum mopane* forms a single-species woodland.

Knob Thorn *Acacia nigrescens* is one of the most widespread and common tree species in the Lowveld and, like Mopane, it may grow in a variety of forms. Pockets of open **Knob Thorn woodland** occur throughout the region, particularly in the west.

Large mammals typical of tree savanna include African Elephant, Buffalo and Sable. Many eagles and vultures construct their nests in tall woodland trees, while Redheaded Weaver, Scops Owl, Woodland Kingfisher, Grey Hornbill and Blackheaded Oriole are characteristic smaller birds.

# Grass Savanna

**Grass savanna** is an open, park-like habitat **dominated by grass** with **widely-spaced trees having broad or flat crowns**. Nutritious grass species dominate and small bushy shrubs are few or absent. This is a sparse habitat in the KNP but popular among tourists in view of the good visibility and the high density of grazing herbivores – Blue Wildebeest and Burchell's Zebra are most common here – and large predators. Characteristic birds are Kori Bustard, Lilacbreasted Roller, Sabota Lark and Longtailed Shrike.

In the KNP grass savanna occurs mostly in a broad band on **clayey soils derived from basalt** between Satara and Crocodile Bridge. Dominant trees are Knob Thorn *Acacia nigrescens*, Umbrella Thorn *Acacia tortilis* and Marula *Sclerocarya birrea*. This grass-dominated habitat is maintained by seasonal grass fires which burn back woody scrub but promote vigorous re-growth of grass; mature trees are protected from fire by thick bark. If fires were prevented, woody plants would encroach.

Pure grasslands are rare in the Lowveld but do occur where repeated seasonal waterlogging prevents tree growth. This happens along so-called **seeplines** where moisture travelling downhill on impervious granite (beneath porous sandy soil) meets the dry but equally impervious clay soils of valley bottoms. Water is forced to the surface and grass prevails at the expense of trees. These **hydromorphic grasslands** follow contours, are usually narrow in width, and are soggy only after substantial rainfalls; they are often characterised by a band of Silver Terminalia *Terminalia sericea* on their upper (dry) fringe. Where seeplines are cut by paths or roads, soil erosion may occur which eventually leads to exposed areas of pale, compacted soil known as **sodic sites**.

# Rocky Outcrops

Between the Drakensberg and its foothills in the west, and the Lebombo Hills in the east, the Lowveld is a mostly flat landscape interrupted in only a few places by rocky outcrops or koppies. Although limited in distribution these rocky habitats support a distinctive variety of specially adapted plants and animals. The different rock types influence not only the shape of the rock formations but also the vegetation.

**Granite** koppies, characterised by balancing boulders and broad domes of peeling rock, are most impressive in the vicinity of Nelspruit and in the KNP around Pretoriuskop restcamp. Similar rock formations occur in the vicinity of Mica and Gravelotte. Among the plants which grow on these koppies are Common Coral Tree *Erythrina lysistemon*, Candelabra Tree *Euphorbia cooperi* and Rock Aloe *Aloe spicata*.

Punda Maria is set among **quartzite** hills which form the eastern arm of the Soutpansberg Mountains. A self-guided trail in this KNP rest-camp allows close examination of rock outcrops and associated plants.

The Lebombo Hills, which separate the Lowveld from the coastal plains of Mozambique, consist of **rhyolite** – a hard rock resistant to weathering – and are characterised by large, reddish boulders. Red Bushwillow *Combretum apiculatum* is the dominant tree species.

Impressive gorges, with sheer cliff faces, are to be found in a few localities such as the Crocodile River Gorge in the Malelane Mountains and Lanner Gorge on the Levuvhu River west of Pafuri.

Klipspringer and Rock Dassie are restricted to rocky outcrops as are Mocking Chat and Freckled Nightjar. Reptiles are particularly common, with Rainbow Skink, Common Flat Lizard and Giant Plated Lizard frequently basking on rockfaces.

# Riverine Forest

**Riverine forest** is typified by **tall, mostly evergreen trees with inter-locking crowns** and a **tangled understorey** dominated by shrubs and creepers. Grasses are sparse or absent. The ready availability of groundwater allows trees to grow close together, but they must compete for light and this results in tall trunks and relatively small crowns.

This forest type is most extensive along the larger rivers such as the Crocodile, Sabie, Olifants and Levuvhu, but thin forest strips also occur along seasonal rivers and drainage lines.

Common riverine trees are the glossy-leaved Matumi *Breonadia salicina*, Jackalberry *Diospyros mespiliformis*, Sycamore Fig *Ficus sycomorus,* Sausage Tree *Kigelia africana*, Knob Thorn *Acacia nigrescens* and Rain Tree *Lonchocarpus capassa*. Wild Date Palm *Phoenix reclinata* and Waterberry *Syzygium cordatum* often grow right at the water's edge. The Ana Tree *Faidherbia albida* is a prominent riverine tree north of the Shingwedzi, while the Fever Tree *Acacia xanthophloea* forms ghostly forests and reaches its greatest size along the Levuvhu at Pafuri. The Potatobush *Phyllanthus reticulatus*, with its evening aroma and the spring flowering Flame Creeper *Combretum microphyllum*, are two sprawling shrubs typical of Lowveld rivers.

Among mammals, Bushbuck and Leopard are most often seen in this habitat while Nyala are restricted to it in the far north of the KNP. Figs and fruiting trees attract Peter's Epauletted Fruit Bat, Green Pigeon, Purplecrested Lourie and Trumpeter Hornbill, while Paradise Flycatcher, Puffback and Heuglin's Robin dwell in the dense foliage. African Fish Eagle usually nests in riverine trees. Butterflies and other insects may be particularly abundant.

# Rivers and Wetlands

There are two major drainage systems in the Lowveld, both having their headwaters in the Drakensberg Mountains and with numerous tributaries, many of which flow only after heavy summer rains.

The **Limpopo System** has the Olifants, Letaba, Levuvhu and Shingwedzi as its major rivers and the Blyde, Timbavati and Selati among the smaller tributaries. The Olifants joins the Limpopo River east of the Lebombo Hills in Mozambique before spilling into the Indian Ocean at Xai-Xai.

The **Inkomati System**, which enters the sea at Maputo, has the Sabie (pictured above), Crocodile and Komati as its major rivers and the Sand and Mbyamiti among the smaller tributaries.

In recent years there has been growing concern over the reduced flow and increased pollution of Lowveld rivers. This has been attributed to a variety of factors including the thirsty timber plantations on the escarpment, intensive irrigation and chemical spraying of cash crops, and sulphuric acid leaching from coal and gold mining. Of the KNP rivers, only the Olifants, Sabie and Crocodile are perennial, while the Letaba and others are now often reduced to a series of pools in the dry season. Smaller tributaries below 600 m have probably always been seasonal.

No natural lakes exist in the Lowveld but a large number of **boreholes and dams** have been created in the KNP; these provide drinking water and aquatic habitats but often lead to overgrazing and erosion as large herbivores congregate permanently in their vicinity. **Marshes**, so attractive to frogs and aquatic birds, have formed around many man-made dams. Hundreds of small **seasonal pans** occur on clayey depressions for a month or more after good summer rains.

# Mammals

The Kruger National Park and adjacent wildlife reserves support an extremely varied mammalian fauna with close to 150 species – from large herbivores to tiny bats – having been recorded. With the successful reintroduction of White and Black Rhino – which were eradicated due to indiscriminate hunting in the 1900's – all of the mammals known to occur in recent times are represented in this large conservation area. Most of the larger mammals have vanished from the escarpment foothills, although certain primates, smaller carnivores, rodents and bats are still common.

In this section, 62 of the more common or conspicuous mammals are featured, with emphasis on the larger herbivores and carnivores. Some species, such as Bushpig and Aardvark are not uncommon, but rarely seen, and are excluded for this reason. Smaller rodents and bats are difficult to identify unless captured – the species featured here are those most frequently seen by casual observers. Where sexes differ, the photograph usually shows the male.

Names used follow those in the region's standard reference work – *The Mammals of the Southern African Subregion* by J. Skinner and R. Smithers (Univ. of Pretoria, 1990) – but hyphens have been deleted. Chris and Tilde Stuart's *Field Guide to the Mammals of Southern Africa* (Struik, 1988) is a more portable yet still comprehensive guide book, while *The Small Mammals of the Kruger National Park* by Pienaar, Rautenbach and De Graaf (National Parks Board, 1980) is a useful regional publication. Other books on mammals and their behaviour are listed on p. 122.

## African Elephant

Huge herbivore. Males are larger than females, with a rounded rather than angular forehead and thicker tusks. Dominant females (matriarchs) lead family units which may combine to form herds of several hundred. Males usually keep to themselves in smaller 'bachelor' groups. Feeds on leaves, bark and grass for over 14 hours of each day and modifies woodlands in the process. Dependent on water.
Height: up to 4 m   Mass: up to 6 000 kg (male)

## Hippopotamus

Huge aquatic herbivore with an almost hairless body, and tiny ears and eyes. The broad mouth has tusk-like teeth. Keeps to water by day, when only its ears, eyes and nostrils protrude above the surface. Comes onto land after dark to feed on grass. Usually found in small herds of 10 to 12. Noisy and aggressive, fearsome clashes ensue between rival males. Young are vulnerable to attack by Nile Crocodile.
Height: 1.5 m   Mass: up to 2 000 kg (male)

## White Rhinoceros

Huge two-horned herbivore with a **hump on its neck**. Much larger than the next species. The **long head is usually carried low to the ground**; the **mouth is broad and squared-off**, allowing it to feed on grass. Occurs singly or in family groups; **most active during the day**. Poor eyesight; calm by nature. Exterminated from the Lowveld by the late 1800s but reintroduced from Zululand in the 1960s.

Height: 1.8 m  Mass: 2 500 kg (male)

## Black Rhinoceros

Massive two-horned herbivore with no hump on its neck. Smaller than the previous species. The **short head is held upright**; the **mouth is pointed with a hooked upper lip**, allowing it to pluck leaves. Occurs singly or in mother and young pairs; **most active at night**. Poor eyesight and a short temper make this a dangerous animal. Shot out in the Lowveld by the 1930s but reintroduced from Zululand.

Height: up to 1.6 m  Mass: up to 1 000 kg

PETER HANCOCK

## Warthog

Sparsely haired pig with curved tusks and wart-like swellings on the face. Males larger with longer tusks and two pairs of 'warts'. The tail is held upright when on the run. Grazes on short grass or digs for tubers on folded knees. Partial to wallowing in mud. Strictly diurnal, retreating to burrow after dark. Sexes live apart, with females caring for piglets. Preyed upon by all larger carnivores but brave in defence.

Height: up to 70 cm  Mass: up to 105 kg (male)

WILDERNESS SAFARIS/COLIN BELL

## Burchell's Zebra

Horse-like herbivore which lives in family units of several mares and their offspring, and a single stallion. Grazer of tall or short grass, and often the first to feed at new growth after fire. May congregate during the rainy season to form large herds – mostly around Satara. Each individual has a unique coat pattern. Call is a bark-like 'gwa-ha'. Lion and Spotted Hyena are the chief predators.

Height: 1.3 m  Mass: up to 340 kg

MARK TENNANT/AFRICAN IMAGES

T B G

## Giraffe

Massive, long-necked herbivore. Feeds on leaves beyond the reach of other browsers. Favours *Acacia* during summer, but switches to Mopane or evergreen trees in the dry season. Social but non-territorial. The small horns of males are bald at the tips; those of females are tufted. Individuals become darker with age. Ageing adults and calves are vulnerable to Lion and Spotted Hyena.

Height: up to 5 m  Mass: up to 1 400 kg (male)

T RF B G

## Buffalo

Massive relative of the domestic cow with a short, sparse coat. Gregarious but non-territorial. Family units may congregate in herds of several hundred or more during the dry season, gathering to feed on nutritious grass. Older bulls often form small groups. Keeps to shade for much of the day, feeding mostly at night. Lion are the main predators but the herd affords good security and protection.

Height: 1.4 m  Mass: up to 700 kg (male)

G T B

## Blue Wildebeest

Large antelope with weak hindquarters and strong forequarters. Adults are grey with a black face and mane and darker creases on sides. Both sexes have horns. Young are tawny coated. Bulls are territorial during breeding season. Gregarious, favouring open country. Bulk grazer of short grass. Lion and Spotted Hyena are the main predators. True migrations no longer occur.

Height: 1.5 m  Horns: 60 cm  Mass: 250 kg (male)

PETER HANCOCK

T G B

## Tsessebe

Large antelope with a distinctive **sloping back**. Short coat is reddish-brown with a maroon sheen and with darker head and upper legs. Both sexes carry short, ringed horns. Small herds of females occupy a home range which overlaps the territory of a male. Selective grazer of short grasses. Said to be the fastest of all antelope. Adults are preyed upon by Lion, the young by other predators.

Height: 1.2 m  Horns: 34 cm  Mass: 140 kg (male)

## Sable Antelope

Horse-like antelope with long mane and swept-back horns. Males are jet-black with contrasting white facial pattern and underbelly; younger females chestnut with shorter, thinner horns. Selective grazer, but will also browse on occasion. Female herds of 10 to 25 range over an area incorporating territory of a dominant bull. May fall prey to Lion, but are attacked with caution.

Height: 1.3 m  Horns: 1 m  Mass: 180-270 kg

B  T

## Roan Antelope

Horse-like antelope with distinctive black and white facial pattern. Sexes are alike with grey to rufous coat having a grizzled appearance; the swept-back horns are thicker and longer in the male. A selective grazer, it favours medium or long grasses; rarely occurring far from water. Small female herds often accompanied by a bull. Susceptible to anthrax, the small KNP population is immunised annually.

Height: 1.4 m  Horns: 75 cm  Mass: up to 300 kg

B  T

## Common Waterbuck

Large, robust antelope less common than might be expected in the region. The coat of long hair is grey-brown and the rump distinctively marked with a **broad white ring**. Only males possess horns. Rarely found far from water, it grazes on alluvial flats or in open areas. Territorial bulls dominate groups of females and their young. Preyed upon by all larger carnivores, particularly Lion.

Height: 1.3 m  Horns: 75 cm  Mass: 260 kg (male)

T  RW  B

## Common Reedbuck

Medium-sized, reddish-brown antelope. Pairs hold territories but boundaries are not well defined. A sharp whistle is the contact and alarm call. The bushy tail and dark band down the forelegs distinguish it from the more gregarious Impala. Only males have horns. Largely nocturnal, but when active during the day keeps mostly to long grass and rank growth near water. Preyed upon by Cheetah and other large predators.

Height: 80-95 cm  Horns: 30 cm  Mass: 60 kg

G  RW

23

B RO T

## Greater Kudu

Large browsing antelope favouring dry woodland. Males carry magnificent spiral horns which attain full length after three years. The coat is grey-brown with six or more thin white stripes. Males have a prominent mane on the shoulders and throat. Females gather in small herds, with males in tow during midwinter rut. Non-breeding males form bachelor herds. Lion is the main predator.

Height: 1.5 m  Horns: 1.2 m  Mass: 250 kg (male)

PETER HANCOCK

RF T EF

## Bushbuck

Primarily nocturnal, this shy antelope may also be active at dusk and dawn. Browses on leaves but also feeds on grass, fruit and flowers. The **pattern of spots and stripes on the fawn-coloured coat is variable**. Only the larger male carries the spiral horns. Common along rivers and often seen on the perimeter of KNP restcamps. May feed in the company of baboons. Leopard is the main predator.

Height: 75 cm  Horns: 26 cm  Mass: 45 kg (male)

RF

## Nyala

Medium-sized antelope confined to the far northern parts of the KNP; most common along the Levuvhu River. **Sexes are distinct**: the larger male has a dark brown coat with a shaggy mane and underbelly, and fawn legs; the shorter-coated female is fawn and lacks horns. Both sexes have several vertical white stripes on their flanks. Chiefly a browser. Occurs in small herds or singly.

Height: 1.1 m  Horns: 60 cm  Mass: 108 kg (male)

B T RF

## Impala

Graceful reddish antelope favouring edges of woodland. **Tuft of black hair on ankle of hind legs is diagnostic**. Males have lyre-shaped horns. Adaptable grazer-browser. Herds of females occupy a home range, and males establish territories during the rut (peak in April-May) with much roaring, snorting and chasing of rivals. Non-breeding males form bachelor herds. Lambs are born in spring. Wild Dog and Cheetah are among the predators.

Height: 90 cm  Horns: 50 cm  Mass: 50 kg (male)

## Common Duiker

Small, grey-brown antelope with heavy build. The **black blaze on the forehead and snout**, and crest of hair on the top of the head are diagnostic. Only the male has horns. Browses on a variety of shrubs and herbs, and may even feed on carrion. Most active at dusk and dawn, and also into the night. Occurs singly or in pairs in a fixed home range in well-wooded habitat. Leopard is the main predator.

Height: 50 cm  Horns: 11 cm  Mass: 18 kg (male)

## Steenbok

Small, brick-red antelope with **large rounded ears**. Only males have horns. Prefers drier open areas with thickets for cover. Mixed feeder of grass, leaves, seed pods and berries. Independent of drinking water. Monogamous and usually seen in pairs. **Active at all hours**, but rests in shade at midday. Young are born at any time of the year. Cheetah and Martial Eagle are among the predators.

Height: 50 cm  Horns: 9 cm  Mass: 11 kg

## Sharpe's Grysbok

Small, stocky antelope with **reddish coat finely streaked with white hairs**. Only males have the short, pointed horns. Mixed feeder of leaves, berries and grass. Usually seen singly but probably lives in pairs in a fixed home range. **Active mostly at night**, but may be seen in early morning or late afternoon. Young are usually born in summer. Most common in northern woodlands.

Height: 50 cm  Horns: 6 cm  Mass: 7.5 kg

## Klipspringer

Small, stocky antelope with grizzled, grey-brown coat. The **prominent orbital glands** and **habit of walking and jumping on hoof tips** are diagnostic. Only the male has a pair of short, pointed horns. Occurs in pairs or family groups on rocky outcrops or cliffs, where it feeds on the leaves of small shrubs and herbs. In the KNP, most common in hilly country around Pretoriuskop and Olifants restcamps.

Length: 85 cm  Height: 60 cm  Mass: 13 kg

RO

## Lion

Very large, sociable cat living in prides of several adult females (often related) and their offspring, and up to three adult males. All defend a territory against rivals. Preys on anything from young Elephant to rodents, but most partial to Buffalo, Zebra and larger antelope. Also pirates kills from other carnivores, and scavenges. Most active at night. The impressive 'roar' may carry for several kilometres.
Height: 1.2 m Length: 2 to 3 m Mass: 220 kg (male)

## Leopard

Large cat with relatively **short legs** and **rosettes of black spots** on tawny coat. Sexes only come together to mate. One or two cubs remain with mother for up to two years. Females have overlapping home ranges; males have larger ranges incorporating those of several females. Elusive and mostly nocturnal. Diverse diet, but small and medium-sized antelope dominate. Kills are stored in trees.
Height: 75 cm Length: 1.8 m Mass: up to 90 kg

## Cheetah

Large elegant cat with **long legs**, greyhound-like frame, **solid black spots** and black 'tear-marks' between eyes and mouth. Adult females often accompanied by two to five cubs for up to two years. Males frequently form coalitions (often brothers) of two or three. Hunts by day (mostly Impala), thereby reducing competition with other predators. Able to sprint at 112 km/h over short distances.
Height: 80 cm Length: 1.8 to 2 m Mass: 50 kg

## Caracal

Medium-sized cat with fawn coat and distinctive **long black tufts on its ears**. The tail is fairly short and thick. The face is distinguished by prominent white lines below the eyes. Sexes are alike. Occurs singly except when female has kittens; up to three being born at any time of the year. **Primarily nocturnal** but may be active during the day in protected areas. Preys on birds and small mammals.
Height: 45 cm Length: 1 m Mass: 8 to 19 kg

## Spotted Hyena

Large, heavily built carnivore with **sloping back**. The coat is fawn with dark blotches becoming fainter with age; young pups are charcoal. Mostly nocturnal. Lives in clans of varying size with larger females dominating males; one female – the matriarch – ranks highest. Clan teams up against rivals, and hunts together (mostly Blue Wildebeest) but members clash over food. Regular scavenger. Very vocal.

Height: 85 cm Length: 1.2 to 1.8 m Mass: 70 kg

## Wild Dog

Slender, long-legged carnivore with large, **rounded ears** and **straight back**. Coat is dappled in dark brown, fawn and white. Sociable, it forms packs of between 6 and 15 adults (plus young-sters) with one dominant pair. Active by day, running down prey (mostly Impala and young of larger antelope) after a chase. The KNP is one of the strong-holds of this endangered species.

Height: 75 cm Length: 1.2 m Mass: 20 to 30 kg

## Blackbacked Jackal

Reddish-yellow jackal with pointed snout and ears, and distinctive black and silver 'saddle'. Pair defends territory and raises three to four pups which remain with parents to help feed the next litter. May congregate to scavenge from larger carcasses. Prey ranges from insects to young Impala. Favours drier, more open areas than the similar **Sidestriped Jackal**. Call is a drawn-out wail.

Height: 38 cm Length: 1 m Mass: 6 to 10 kg

## Honey Badger (Ratel)

Stout, short-legged carnivore boldly marked in black and silvery-white. Usually seen alone, but likely to live in monogamous pairs. A powerful and avid digger, it uses its strong claws to unearth mole rats and other prey. Climbs trees for honey and bee larvae, but its relationship with Greater Honeyguide is contentious. Strips bark off trees in search of reptiles. May enter camps to scavenge.

Height: 30 cm Length: 1 m Mass: 8 to 14 kg

C & T STUART

T  B

## Civet

Robust, raccoon-like carnivore with a distinctive **black mask**, boldly marked coat and ringed tail. Long spinal crest is raised when alarmed. Nocturnal, but may be seen prowling sand roads and open areas after dark. Diet is diverse and includes millipedes, snakes and the fruit of the Wild Date Palm. Solitary and territorial. Frequently scent-marks and creates specific latrine sites.

Height: 40 cm  Length: 1.2 m  Mass: 9 to 15 kg

LEX HES

RF  B  EF

## Largespotted Genet

Slim, short-legged carnivore with spotted coat and long, ringed tail, usually **black-tipped**. Spots vary in colour from black to rusty. Strictly nocturnal; most often seen in trees or running across roads. Solitary and territorial. Preys on a wide variety of creatures from insects to nestling birds. The similar **Smallspotted Genet** differs in having a **white-tipped tail** and pure black spots.

Height: 45 cm  Length: 1 m  Mass: 2 to 3 kg

LEX HES

RF  EF  G

## Whitetailed Mongoose

Large mongoose with long **bushy tail tipped in white**. The overall body colour is grey with the legs and feet being darker. Strictly nocturnal, it often forages along roads or in open areas and is therefore commonly encountered after dark. Occurs singly or in small family groups within a fixed home range. Prey includes large insects, scorpions, rodents, birds' eggs, frogs and fallen fruit.

Length: 1.4 m (incl. 45 cm tail)  Mass: up to 5 kg

G  B  T

## Banded Mongoose

Stocky mongoose with distinctive vertical bars on back and flanks of grizzled coat. Gregarious, living in troops of up to 35 with up to four breeding females and males. Active by day within a defined home range. Packs move together but individuals forage separately and guard food jealously. Invertebrates, small reptiles and birds' eggs are favoured. Den is in a termite mound within a thicket.

Length: 55 cm  Mass: 1 to 1.5 kg

## Dwarf Mongoose

Tiny mongoose with glossy reddish coat. Lives in troops of about ten (but up to 30) with a single breeding pair. Active by day within a defined home range. Pack moves together but individuals pursue invertebrate prey independently. Den is often in an exposed termite mound. At first glance it could be confused with **Tree Squirrel** (p. 31). Preyed upon by eagles and other birds of prey.
Length: 35 cm  Mass: 220 to 350 g

## Slender Mongoose

Small carnivore with **reddish coat** and **very long, black-tipped tail**. Often seen crossing roads with its tail held aloft. Occurs singly in a variety of habitats, including gardens adjacent to rocky outcrops and parks. Most of its time is spent on the ground, but this mongoose is also an adept tree climber. Its diet includes insects, birds' eggs and lizards. Active mostly by day.
Length: 60 cm (incl. 27 cm tail)  Mass: 650 g

## Shortsnouted Elephant Shrew

Small insectivore which – despite its name – has a long snout (albeit shorter than that of other elephant shrews). The reddish-yellow coat is flecked with black, the underbelly and throat are white, and the large eyes are ringed in white or buff. Keeps to well-wooded areas with longer grass, including Mopane scrub. Diurnal, but most active at dawn.
Length: 21 cm (incl. 10 cm tail)  Mass: 44 g
ss: Fourtoed Elephant Shrew (far north only)

C & T STUART

## Lesser Red Musk Shrew

Tiny nocturnal insectivore with pointed snout and small, rounded ears. A voracious predator of small insects and worms, it often eats the equivalent of its own body weight each night. May be seen around buildings, where it feeds on insects drawn to lights. Males engage in fierce fights, squealing loudly in the process. Young clasp mother's tail when on the move.
Length: 13 cm (incl. 5 cm tail)  Mass: 16 g
ss: Tiny Musk Shrew; Reddish-grey Musk Shrew

NATIONAL PARKS BOARD OF S.A.

## Chacma Baboon

Large, dog-like primate with shaggy, grey-brown coat and long bare snout. Males much larger than females, which have naked buttocks changeable in colour and shape depending upon sexual condition. Babies often ride on mother's back. Lives in troops of up to 100, with adult males in strict hierarchy. Feeds on a wide variety of plants and animals. Often associates with Impala. Very vocal.

Length: up to 1.6 m (male)  Mass: 32 kg (male)

IAN SUTHERLAND/AFRICAN IMAGES

## Vervet Monkey

Inquisitive, agile primate with grizzled grey coat, distinctive black face and long tail. Lives in troops of up to 20, comprised of adult females and offspring, and accompanied by one or more mature males. A strict hierarchy exists between females. Readily comes to ground but retreats to trees, and sleeps on branches at night. Feeds on a variety of fruit and small animals. Often enters camps and gardens.

Length: 1 to 1.3 m  Mass: 4 to 5 kg

## Greater Bushbaby

Small nocturnal primate with large eyes and long, **thick bushy tail**; somewhat cat-like in appearance. It is more than twice the size of the next species. Bounds through trees with great agility. Groups occupy a home range, their presence often betrayed by their **eerie wailing call** – similar to that of a human child. Sleeps in a tree hole or thicket by day. Fruit, acacia gum and insects are the main food.

Length: 80 cm (incl. 40 cm tail)  Mass: 1.5 kg

LEX HES

## Lesser Bushbaby

Tiny nocturnal primate with **huge bulging eyes** and long fluffy tail. Bounds through trees with great agility. Female and off-spring occupy a home range; males have larger territories incorporating the ranges of several females. Aerial pathways are scent-marked with urine. Family groups sleep together in day nest. Feeds on insects and gum of acacia trees. Calls include a high-pitched wail. Restless.

Length: 35 cm (incl. 20 cm tail)  Mass: 150 g

## Scrub Hare

The **long ears**, **short bushy tail** and **grizzled grey coat** prevent confusion with the next species. Nocturnal in habits but may be flushed from resting place during the day; sometimes active in the late afternoon or early morning. Runs in a typical zig-zag fashion when disturbed. Feeds primarily on grass. Raises litters of one to three each year. Predators include Giant Eagle Owl, Caracal and Leopard.
Length: 53 cm  Mass: 2 to 4 kg

EF  G  B

## Rock Dassie

Compact, short-eared mammal with **no obvious tail**. Active by day, it frequently basks in the sun, particularly in early mornings and on cool winter days. Colonies comprise several family units. Latrines are characterised by white and brown urine streaks on rocks, and **spherical pellets**. The diet includes grass, leaves and berries. May climb into trees to feed. Calls with a sharp bark.
Length: 50 cm  Mass: 4 to 5 kg

MARK TENNANT/AFRICAN IMAGES

RO

## Porcupine

Large nocturnal rodent with **long black and white quills**. Vegetarian, it is an avid digger, feeding primarily on roots and tubers. Tree bark is also favoured. Days are spent in a burrow. Its presence may be detected by gnaw marks on tree trunks and discarded quills. The quills may be raised in alarm, and are used in defence against predators such as Leopard and Lion.
Length: 75 to 100 cm  Mass: 10 to 24 kg

LEX HES

T  EF  B  RO

## Tree Squirrel

Small, bushy-tailed rodent with grey to yellow-brown coat, paler underneath. Keeps mostly to trees but runs nimbly on the ground. Most abundant in mature Mopane woodland, but occurs in most habitats. Usually seen singly or in small family groups. Males may be territorial. A chattering, bird-like call is made in alarm and often indicates the presence of an eagle, snake or other predator.
Length: 35 cm  Mass: 100 to 250 g

EF  B  T

## Common Slitfaced Bat

Small bat characterised by a longitudinal slit down the face (which, however, is difficult to see). The wings are rounded and the tail is broad with a notched tip. But the most obvious feature is the **long and conspicuous ears**. Roosts in colonies of several hundred in caves or man-made structures, or holes in Baobab trees. Rarely emerges until well after dark.

Length: 10 cm  Wingspan: 24 cm  Mass: 11 g

B  RO  EF

## Little Freetailed Bat

Very small, insectivorous bat occurring in a wide variety of habitats. Uniform brown to sandy-fawn in colour, with large ears and a wrinkled, mastiff-like face. The distinctive feature is the **small thin tail which protrudes beyond the tail membrane**. Gregarious, it roosts by day in tree holes, palm fronds, roofs or other man-made structures.

Length: 9 cm  Wingspan: 24 cm  Mass: 11 g
ss: Angola Freetailed Bat (11 cm, 15 g)

B  RF

## Schliefen's Bat

Tiny bat with no outstanding features. Differs from the Little Freetailed Bat in having the tail spanned by a tail membrane, and from the Banana Bat in being **pale fawn or reddish brown on the underparts**. The wing membranes are darker than the body. Roosts singly or in small groups in hollow trees or crevices in buildings and rocks, emerging at dusk to hunt small flying insects.

Length: 7.5 cm Wingspan: 18 cm  Mass: 4 g

B  RO  EF

## Banana Bat

Tiny bat with no outstanding features – also known as a pipistrelle. The **body and wing membranes are dark brown**; the tail is spanned by a tail membrane. Most common in banana plantations and in gardens where *Strelitzia* plants are grown; groups of up to six roost by day in the unfurled leaves of these plants. Emerges at dusk to hunt small flying insects.

Length: 7.5 cm  Wingspan: 19 cm  Mass: 4 g

EF

32

## Peter's Epauletted Fruit Bat

Large, fruit-eating bat. Males call with a resounding 'ping' – a characteristic night sound in the region. The coat is grey-yellow with **two pairs of distinctive white spots in front of, and behind, the ears**. Males have tufts of white hair on the shoulders which are erected into 'epaulettes' during display. Roosts within dense foliage or under thatch. Navigates by sight. Figs are the favoured food.

Length: 15 cm  Wingspan: 56 cm  Mass: 100 g

## Mauritian Tomb Bat

Medium-sized, insectivorous bat with **silky grey head and back, and snow-white underparts**; the wing membranes are pale grey. The tail is free from the tail membrane but does not extend beyond it. Roosts singly or in pairs; often in exposed sites such as brick walls and tree trunks. Thought to have better eyesight than other insectivorous bats and may hunt on overcast days.

Length: 10 cm  Wingspan: 34 cm  Mass: 28 g

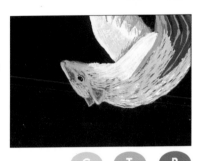

## Common Molerat

Small, short-legged rodent with **tiny eyes, hidden ears** and **protruding teeth**. This is the creature responsible for the mounds of earth which appear on lawns and sports fields. Abundant, but rarely seen due to its underground life-style. It spends the daylight hours below ground, where it burrows through the soil in search of roots and bulbs. It may emerge from its burrow system at night.

Length: 15 cm  Mass: up to 150 g

## Greater Cane Rat

Large, beaver-like rodent with coarse grizzled coat. The head is small in relation to the body, and the ears are tiny. The short tail is almost naked. Lives in small colonies in reedbeds, feeding on stems and roots of sedges, reeds and grasses; often abundant in sugarcane fields. Regular pathways are used. Nocturnal, but sometimes active at dusk. Predators include Rock Python and Leopard.

Length: 65 to 80 cm  Mass: 3 to 5 kg

NATIONAL PARKS BOARD OF S.A.

**B  G  EF**

## Singlestriped Mouse

Small rodent with upperparts varying in colour from grey to fawn. The **single dark stripe** running down the centre of the back is diagnostic. Diurnal, and therefore the most frequently seen rodent. Spends all its time on the ground and is often seen running across tracks and along roadsides. Grass seeds are the main food, and numbers fluctuate in relation to rainfall. Preyed upon by smaller raptors.
Length: 27 cm (incl. 15 cm tail)  Mass: 60 g

C & T STUART

**B  G  EF**

## Multimammate Mouse

Fairly small, long-tailed rodent with **large rounded ears** and grey-brown coat. Larger than the similar House Mouse. Nocturnal and omnivorous. May occur in houses and buildings. Its name refers to the extraordinary number of teats – up to 12 pairs – possessed by the female, a factor which allows this to be the most rapidly reproducing mammal in Africa. Population explosions may occur.
Length: 24 cm (incl. 11 cm tail)  Mass: 60 g

C & T STUART

**EF**

## House Mouse *

Small, long-tailed rodent with **large rounded ears** and grey-brown coat. Nocturnal and omnivorous. Dependent upon the dwellings and refuse of humans. Untidy nests are made of paper and other rubbish. Breeds prolifically. Thought to have originated in northern Europe, local populations probably expanded from ports such as Cape Town and Durban.
Length: 16 cm (incl. 9 cm tail)  Mass: 18 g

NATIONAL PARKS BOARD OF S.A.

**T  RF  EF**

## Woodland Dormouse

Small, silvery-grey rodent with white underparts and **bushy, squirrel-like tail**. It is at home in the branches of trees (especially acacias) and may also frequent structures around homesteads. Strictly nocturnal, its diet includes insects, spiders and seeds. A substantial **nest of fine grass**, lichen and leaves is constructed within a tree hole, rock crevice or similar cavity.
Length: 16 cm (incl. 7 cm tail)  Mass: 30 g

## Red Veld Rat

Small, large-eyed rodent with reddish-brown fur streaked in black on the forehead and back; the underparts are off-white. The **tail is long and scaly**, the ears large and rounded. Occurs in small colonies which construct ground nests of twigs and grass, or excavate burrows at the base of a bush. Strictly nocturnal, it feeds on seeds. The similar **Namaqua Rock Mouse** is restricted to rocky places.

Length: 28 cm (incl. 15 cm tail)  Mass: 75 g

## Angoni Vlei Rat

Short-tailed rodent with a blunt nose, shaggy fur and round ears. Occurs in dense vegetation near water. Active during both night and day, making use of runs and tunnels in order to reach feeding sites. Grass roots, reeds and sedges are favoured. Preyed upon by Serval and various raptors. Although only visible when skulls are examined, the upper incisors are deeply grooved.

Length: 30 cm (incl. 8 cm tail)  Mass: 100 to 250 g

## House Rat *

Large, long-tailed rodent with rounded ears and grey-black coat. Its completely **naked tail** is diagnostic. It lives in close proximity to man, particularly in warehouses and storerooms where untidy nests are made with a variety of odds and ends. Like the House Mouse, this species arrived first at South Africa's ports before spreading inland to major towns. Omnivorous and destructive.

Length: 37 cm (incl. 20 cm tail)  Mass: 150 g

## Bushveld Gerbil

Reddish-brown rodent with pure white underparts and diagnostic dark stripe running down the length of its sparsely haired tail. Nocturnal, living in small colonies. Most common in areas of sandy soil where burrows are excavated. Feeds on seeds and insects. As with other gerbils, this species is a vector for the plague virus, but it rarely lives near man so contact with fleas is rare.

Length: 28 cm (incl. 15 cm tail)  Mass: 70 g

35

# Birds

The Lowveld is extremely rich in birds with over 500 species having been recorded in the Kruger National Park and adjacent reserves. The density of large eagles and vultures, and the abundance of colourful rollers, bee-eaters, kingfishers and hornbills are among the highlights of what is one of the best birdwatching regions in Africa. In addition to the wildlife reserves, towns such as Nelspruit – with its excellent botanical garden and leafy suburbs – also support a wide variety of birds, some of which are uncommon in the KNP.

More bird species occur during the summer months, when migrants from further afield are present, and smaller songbirds are most vocal at this time. In winter, however, the sparser vegetation is an advantage when looking for bush birds. Suitable habitat for waterfowl is limited, but the numerous artificial dams and waterholes in the KNP attract several species of heron, stork and duck. When in wildlife reserves, it is advisable to spend time walking around restcamps, as the occurrence of water and flowering plants attract many species, especially in the dry winter months. When driving, the most useful tip is to stop and turn the car motor off at regular intervals, so as to hear birds calling.

Due to space restrictions, a number of fairly common species have had to be left out of this section; an attempt has been made, however, to cover as broad a spectrum of birds as possible. Species are arranged in such a way that those which could be confused appear on the same spread. *Sasol Birds of Southern Africa* (Struik, 1993) is the most comprehensive field guide – a list of other useful books appears on p. 122.

## Reed Cormorant

Medium-sized, black waterbird with a long tail and **red eyes**. Immature birds have an off-white breast. In common with other cormorants, the feathers are not waterproof and it regularly perches with its wings outstretched so that they may dry. Fish are caught underwater. Breeds colonially in large trees or in reedbeds, often in the company of herons or storks.

Length: 52 cm   ss: African Finfoot (red bill and legs)

## African Darter

Large, dark brown waterbird with a long neck – often held in an S-bend shape – and a sharp, pointed bill. Breeding adults have a rufous throat edged in white. The wings are held outstretched to dry. Dives for fish, which are speared before being brought to the surface. Often swims with only the neck and head above water, leading to its alternative name of Snakebird.

Length: 80 cm   ss: Whitebreasted Cormorant

## Greenbacked Heron

Small dark heron with short neck and yellow-green legs. The back is dark grey-green with buffy edges to wing feathers, the crown black, and the underside blue-grey. Immature birds are streaked on the throat and face, and spotted with white on the wings. Often draws attention to itself by the harsh croaking call uttered in flight. Readily perches on exposed branches. Forages at water's edge.
Length: 40 cm  ss: Dwarf Bittern (25 cm)

## Cattle Egret

Small, all-white egret with relatively short neck and legs. When breeding, the crown, mantle and chest are adorned in buffy plumes, the bill and legs are coral-pink and the toes black. Non-breeding birds have a yellow bill and olive-brown legs and toes. Gregarious, feeding on dry land in the company of large mammals which disturb insect prey. Roosts and breeds in reedbeds or trees.
Length: 54 cm  ss: Little Egret (65 cm)

## Great White Egret

Large, all-white egret with long neck. The **legs and toes are black at all times**. Prior to breeding, the bill is black and the bare skin around eyes lime-green. The bill and bare skin is yellow during and after breeding. Favours marshes where it usually occurs singly, or in the company of other species. Feeds on fish, frogs and rodents. A stick nest is built within reedbeds or on the branches of a dead tree.
Length: 75 cm  ss: Yellowbilled Egret (66 cm)

## Grey Heron

Large, pale grey heron with **white head and neck**, and long yellow bill. A bold black streak runs above and behind the eye to form a small crest. In flight, the **underwing is uniform grey**. Usually seen alone on floodplains or the verges of rivers and lagoons where it hunts for frogs and fish. The nest is a platform of reeds and sticks, built in a tree or reedbed.
Length: 100 cm  ss: Blackheaded Heron (underwing grey and black, forages mostly on dry land)

## Goliath Heron

Massive, slate-grey heron with rufous head, neck and underparts. The immature is paler with white on the throat extending to the chest. Usually nests among reeds away from other species. Occurs singly or in pairs, often standing motionless at water's edge. Large fish and crabs are the main food but baby crocodiles may also be taken. Flies with slow, deep wingbeats; the neck is tucked in.

Length: 1.4 m   ss: Purple Heron (90 cm)

## White Stork

Large white stork with black flight feathers and red legs. Told from the previous species by its straight **red bill**, white face and **white tail**. Like most other storks, the legs may be washed white with excreta. Gathers in flocks – often in the company of Abdim's Stork – to feed on grasshoppers on dry land. Often soars in thermals. Non-breeding **summer migrant** from Europe.

Length: 1.2 m

## Yellowbilled Stork

Large white stork with black flight feathers and red legs. Told from the next species by its slightly down-curved **yellow bill**, bare **red face** and **black tail**. When breeding, the mantle and wings are washed with pink. The immature is dull grey-white with yellowish legs and bill. Feeds in shallow water, taking frogs and insects. During the breeding season the back and wing coverts are pinkish.

Length: 1 m

## Marabou Stork

Massive grey stork with white underparts, enormous bill and naked head and neck. The pink face is sparsely covered with bristles. A sausage-shaped pouch hangs beneath the throat. The legs are grey, but often washed white with excreta. Feeds on carrion and attracted in large numbers to fish stranded in shrinking pools. Frequently seen on the outskirts of camps in the KNP.

Length: 1.5 m

## Saddlebilled Stork

Large stork with pied plumage, and black
legs with pink toes and 'knee' joints. The
massive red bill is divided by a black bar
and has a yellow, saddle-shaped shield on
top. Males differ from females in having
black (not yellow) eyes and a small yellow
wattle at the base of the bill. Immature
lacks any red on bill or legs. Feeds in
shallow water, in pairs or family groups.
Nest is built in a tree-top away from water.
Length: 1.4 m

WILDERNESS SAFARIS/COLIN BELL

## Abdim's (Whitebellied) Stork

Small, black and white stork with purplish
sheen to neck, mantle and wing coverts.
The legs are pale mauve with pink toes
and 'knee' joints; the bill is ochre. Blue
and red skin encircles the dark eye.
Gregarious, large flocks gather in short
grassland to feed on grasshoppers and
other insects. Often soars in thermals during the day. Nomadic, non-breeding
**summer migrant** from tropical Africa.
Length: 75 cm  ss: Black Stork (1.2 m)

EF   G

## Hamerkop

Plain brown bird with distinctive,
**backward-pointing crest** and pointed bill
giving the head a hammer-like shape.
Occurs singly or in pairs. Often spends
long periods standing motionless at the
water's edge, waiting for opportunities
to catch frogs and other aquatic life.
A huge, dome-shaped nest of twigs and
mud is built in the fork of a large tree.
The call is a squeaky 'kiepp'.
Length: 55 cm

RW

## Hadeda Ibis

Heavy-bodied, short-legged ibis, and one
of the noisiest of birds. The plumage is
predominantly olive-green, but a metallic
sheen of purple and emerald is present
on the shoulders. Forages most often
beneath shady trees where insects and
worms are extracted from the soil or
among leaves. Groups fly to and from
tree-top roosts at dawn and dusk. A stick
nest is built within the canopy of a tree.
Length: 75 cm

EF   RF

## Egyptian Goose

Large, chestnut and fawn goose with a dark mask around the eyes. In flight, the black and white wings with emerald-green panels are diagnostic. Occurs in pairs or small groups along rivers and at dams, but may congregate in sizeable flocks. Feeds mostly on grass on dry land after dark. Noisy and aggressive during the breeding season. Breeds in a large tree hole or in a Hamerkop nest.
Length: 70 cm

## Redbilled Teal

Small duck with diagnostic **crimson-red bill** and **dark cap**. Avoids rivers. Rather inconspicuous due to its habit of foraging among vegetation. May gather in large flocks. Prefers shallow water, and is usually the first to arrive at flooded grasslands after rain. Food consists of grass seeds, grain and small aquatic creatures. Eggs are laid in a bowl nest among sedges or grass.
Length: 48 cm   ss: Yellowbilled Duck (54 cm)

## Whitefaced Duck

Long-necked duck with an upright stance. It often draws attention to itself with its flute-like call. The distinctive white face, chestnut neck, and black and white barred flanks are diagnostic. May gather in large flocks at dams and pans, spending much of its time resting at the water's edge. Feeds on aquatic tubers and seeds. A nest bowl is made among grass, often far from water.
Length: 48 cm   ss: Fulvous Duck

## African Finfoot

Unusual, cormorant-like bird with **red bill and legs** which are distinctive when it leaves the water. Male has a dark face; the female has a white throat and breast. Swims along the edges of rivers beneath overhanging trees. Feeds mostly on frogs and invertebrates. Secretive but regularly seen along the Sabie River in the vicinity of Skukuza, and on the Crocodile River in the Lowveld Botanical Garden.
Length: 63 cm

## Dabchick (Little Grebe)

Small waterbird, superficially resembling a duck. The **chestnut neck and pale spot at the base of the bill** – of breeding adults – are diagnostic, as is the habit of repeatedly diving below the surface of the water. Small fish, crabs and frogs are caught underwater. May be found on any stretch of open water, but favours dams and pans. A loud trill is the call, often uttered during courtship.
Length: 20 cm

## Black Crake

Small, jet-black bird with **lime-yellow bill and bright red legs**. Inconspicuous and shy but much less so than other crakes. Often located by its call – a harsh throaty warble, frequently a duet between a pair. The very long toes allow it to run across floating vegetation. Small aquatic insects are the main food. The nest is well hidden amongst reeds or sedges.
Length: 21 cm ss: African Crake

## Moorhen

Black waterbird with **red frontal shield and bill with a yellow tip**. The legs and feet are bright yellow and there is a thin white streak running down each flank. Smaller, and with a lighter build than the previous species with which it often shares the same habitat. When out of the water, the short tail is repeatedly flicked up and down to reveal snow-white under-feathers. Feeds on aquatic plants.
Length: 33 cm

LEX HES

## African Jacana

Slender, rust-red bird with white face and neck, and **pale blue shield of bare skin on the forehead**. Extremely long toes enable it to walk on floating vegetation and waterlily leaves. The immature has a white eye-stripe and white under-parts and could be confused with the next species. Found on water bodies with emergent vegetation. Feeds on aquatic insects. Occurs singly or in small noisy groups.
Length: 28 cm

LEX HES

41

 RW  EF

# Blacksmith Plover

Black, grey and white plover with dark red eyes. The long legs are grey-black. Occurs in pairs or family groups in open habitats, often near water. Like other plovers, it lays its camouflaged eggs on bare ground, relying on egg and nestling camouflage for protection. When nests are threatened, the parents rise into the air above the intruders, chanting their metallic 'tink-tink' call.
Length: 30 cm

 G  EF

# Crowned Plover

Sandy-brown plover with a white under-belly, and **black and white crown**. The **long legs are red**. Occurs in short grass-land; in pairs when breeding, or flocks during winter. Camouflaged eggs are laid on the ground. In defence of eggs and young adults circle above intruders, dive-bombing and calling loudly; they may feign injury in order to distract predators from their nest.
Length: 30 cm  ss: Lesser Blackwinged Plover (22 cm)

RW

# Whitecrowned Plover

Grey-brown plover with a **white breast** and underbelly, and **white crown**. The **long legs are yellow**. In flight the upper and lower wings are mostly white. A pair of fleshy wattles hangs below the bill. Occurs in pairs or small groups on exposed sandflats along larger rivers; most common on the Olifants and Levuvhu rivers in the KNP. The similar **Wattled Plover** has a grey breast.
Length: 30 cm  ss: Wattled Plover (35 cm)

RW

# Water Dikkop

Nocturnal, plover-like bird occurring on the edges of lagoons and rivers. The large **yellow eyes and long yellow legs** are distinctive. The streaked upperparts, grey wing panel and **white wing bar** distinguish it from the larger **Spotted Dikkop** (which is found in dry habitats). Occurs in pairs or small groups. The call is a plaintive whistle made after dark. Feeds on small aquatic creatures.
Length: 40 cm  ss: Spotted Dikkop (44 cm)

42

## Wood Sandpiper

Small, grey-brown wader with fairly long yellow legs and a thin bill. The **dark back is boldly spotted in white** and the white eye-stripe extends to the back of the head. Common **summer migrant** usually found on mudflats and in shallow water. Many individuals may forage around a single body of water, but they tend to space themselves out. In flight, the **white rump** is conspicuous.

Length: 20 cm  ss: Marsh Sandpiper (23 cm)

## Common Sandpiper

Small, grey-brown wader with fairly short, grey-green legs and thin bill. The **plain brown back** and **white shoulder patch in the shape of an inverted C** are diagnostic. Common **summer migrant** usually found foraging alone on mud-flats or flooded grassland. When walking, the tail is constantly bobbed up and down. In flight, the long **white wing bars** are conspicuous.

Length: 20 cm  ss: Ruff (26 cm)

## Threebanded Plover

Small plover with plain brown back contrasting with white underparts, and **red eye-ring**. Its name is something of a misnomer, as there are only **two black chest bands**. Occurs singly or in pairs on mudflats where it searches busily for small insects and worms. Frequently confiding. Often associates with migrant waders in summer.

Length: 18 cm  ss: Kittlitz's Plover (buff breast); Whitefronted Plover (pale grey back)

## Blackwinged Stilt

Slender, black and white wader with **extraordinarily long red legs**, and thin pointed bill. Immature birds have grey smudges on the head. Favours mudflats and shallow water, often feeding in the company of larger storks and herons. Frequently bends over to probe the mud for worms and insect larvae. Prone to seasonal movement depending upon water levels.

Length: 38 cm

## Kori Bustard

Massive, grey-brown bustard with white underparts and neck finely barred in grey. Weighing up to 19 kg, it is said to be the heaviest flying bird. A small black crest protrudes from the back of the head. Favours open country where it strides slowly in search of insects, lizards and seeds. The dramatic courtship display includes the puffing-out of the neck feathers. Eggs are laid near a grass tuft. Length: 1.3 m

LEX HES

## Redcrested Korhaan

Small slender bustard with speckled brown back marked with diagnostic **white V-patterns**, and black underbelly. Male has a grey neck. Despite its name, the red crest is only visible in displaying males, which also engage in dramatic aerial courtship displays. The call is a drawn-out, piping whistle. Occurs in pairs. Shy, but relies on camouflage and often stands motionless when detected. Length: 50 cm

LANCE IMAGE

## Blackbellied Korhaan

Medium-sized bustard with fawn back blotched in dark brown. The male may be told from the previous species by the **black line extending from the belly to the chin**, and by the white cheek patches. The **female has a white belly**. Occurs singly or in pairs. Territorial males frequently stand on top of termite mounds to utter their strange, frog-like call – a grunt followed by a pause and a pop. Length: 64 cm

LEX HES

## Ostrich

Huge flightless bird with long neck and legs. Males are predominantly black with white wings and ginger tail plumes; when breeding the pink scales on the shins become red. Females are dull grey-brown. Occurs in pairs when breeding, but thereafter in small flocks. Often associates with antelope. Wary, and able to run at great speeds. Most common in open areas such as Satara in the KNP. Height: 2 m

## Swainson's Francolin

Dark brown francolin with streaked plumage and **bare red skin around the eyes**. The upper bill and legs are black. The harsh, crowing call is often made from a termite mound or branch of a tree. Prefers denser vegetation than the Natal Francolin, and is most common in the central parts of the KNP. Nervous and quick to retreat into cover. Feeds mostly on berries, seeds and insects.
Length: 38 cm

B  G

## Natal Francolin

Dark brown francolin with cream-fawn underparts mottled and streaked in brown. The only francolin in the region with **red bill *and* legs**; the base of the bill is yellow. Occurs in pairs or family groups in dense vegetation, but regularly venturing onto roads or lawns at camps. The call is a loud screeching din, heard most often at dusk and dawn. Feeds on berries, seeds and insects.
Length: 35 cm   ss: Shelly's Francolin (33 cm)

LEX HES

EF  RF  B

## Crested Francolin

Fawn, rust and cream francolin with a broad **white eye-stripe** and dark line through the eye. The crown is dark, the bill grey and the legs are pink-orange. Occurs in pairs or family parties, often coming out onto sand tracks. Call is a rattling 'chee-chatla' repeated excitedly at dawn, less often at dusk. Termites and other insects are the chief food. Eggs are laid on the ground amongst vegetation.
Length: 33 cm   ss: Coqui Francolin (24 cm)

T  B

## Helmeted Guineafowl

Distinctive, charcoal-grey bird profusely spotted in white. The bare facial skin is predominantly blue, with a variable amount of red around the eyes. A horny casque – in the shape of a helmet – sits on the crown. Occurs in flocks in dry woodland, and is particularly abundant around dams and along rivers. Feeds on termites, beetles and seeds. Eggs are laid on the ground amongst dense vegetation.
Length: 56 cm   ss: Crested Guineafowl (Pafuri)

LEX HES

EF  B  G

45

## Whitebacked Vulture

Large, drab brown vulture with a **long, almost bare neck**. Adults become paler with age, ranging from brown to blonde. The **white back** of adults is visible only in flight. The immature is dark brown with pale streaks and lacks the white back. Gregarious scavenger; hundreds may gather to feed at a large carcass. Noisy and quarrelsome. Stick nests are built on the top of a tall tree.
Length: 95 cm ss: Cape Vulture (1.2 m, pale eyes)

## Hooded Vulture

Small, dark brown vulture with a **long thin bill**. The face and throat of the adult is pink, and the leggings white. Immature has a pale grey face and dark brown leggings. Lives in pairs and is usually outnumbered by other vultures at carcasses. Small flocks may gather at hunting camps. Uniformly dark in flight, it may be confused with the next species. Nest is built in the fork of an evergreen tree.
Length: 70 cm

## Lappetfaced Vulture

Huge, dark brown vulture with a pink face and massive, horn-coloured bill. The adult has a **white breast with dark streaks** and **white leggings**. Immature has a pale face and little or no white on the body. Usually in pairs, but dominates other vultures at carcasses. May kill small animals for itself. In flight the **white leggings and 'armpits'** are diagnostic. Nests on top of a low tree.
Length: 1 m

## Whiteheaded Vulture

Large black vulture with diagnostic **orange bill** and pale blue cere. The adult has a white top to the head and white leggings; the face is flushed pink when excited. Female differs from male in having white secondary feathers on the wing. Immature has a brown head and leggings but also has an orange bill. Occurs in singly or in pairs. May catch its own prey in addition to feeding on carrion. Nests on top of a tall tree.
Length: 80 cm

## African Fish Eagle

Large, rust-brown eagle with **snow-white head and chest**. Sexes alike but female larger. Immature is mottled in brown and white. Resident of rivers and wetlands. Often located by its evocative 'kyow-kow-kow' call. Pairs often perch within sight of each other in tall trees, swooping down to grasp fish from the water, or to 'pirate' a meal from another bird. Nests below the canopy of a tall tree.

Length: 63 to 73 cm  ss: Osprey (55 to 65 cm)

## African Hawk Eagle

Medium-sized eagle with charcoal-grey back and white underparts streaked in black. Yellow feet protrude from the fully feathered legs. Female is considerably larger than male. In the flight, the **dark terminal tail bar** and white wing 'windows' are distinctive. Immature has rufous head and underparts. Usually seen in pairs. The nest is built below the canopy of a large tree.

Length: 66 to 74 cm

## Martial Eagle

Huge eagle with **white breast finely spotted in brown,** and dark brown back and head peaked with a small crest. The eyes are yellow. In flight, the **dark underwings** are diagnostic. Immature is pure white below and pale grey above. Preys on animals up to the size of Steenbok but favours monitors and guineafowl. Nests below the canopy of a tall tree.

Length: 80 cm  ss: Blackbreasted Snake Eagle (65 cm, white underwings, unspotted breast)

## Longcrested Eagle

Small black eagle with **distinctive crest of floppy feathers**. The feet, cere and eyes are pale yellow. Male differs from female in having unblotched white leggings. In flight the boldly barred tail and white wing 'windows' are distinctive. Immature has short crest. Rare in the KNP but frequently seen in the vicinity of Nelspruit and Tzaneen. The nest is often built in a tall *Eucalyptus* tree.

Length: 52 to 58 cm

JOHN CARLYON

## Tawny Eagle

Large eagle with variable plumage. Some birds are rich rufous in colour, others pale blonde, but most are tawny-brown. Females are often darker than males. The feet and cere are yellow and the **leggings are shaggy**. Preys and scavenges on a variety of small animals and often pirates kills of other birds. Nest is built on the top of a tall tree.

Length: 70 cm  ss: Steppe Eagle (75 cm, summer migrant); Lesser Spotted Eagle (65 cm, summer)

## Wahlberg's Eagle

Small eagle with plumage varying from dark brown to blonde, but usually medium brown. When perched, the diagnostic **small crest** is visible at the back of the head. In flight, the comparatively long **tail is usually held closed** (rather than fanned). Preys on small animals from gamebirds to flying termites, but not known to scavenge. **Summer migrant**, nesting below the canopy of a tree.

Length: 58 cm  ss: Booted Eagle (50 cm)

## Brown Snake Eagle

Large brown eagle with characteristic **upright posture** and **large rounded head**. The big **eyes are bright yellow**. The grey-white legs are unfeathered. In flight, the pale underwings contrast sharply with the brown body, and the tail is boldly barred. Immature is sandy-brown. Snakes, including puff adders and cobras, are the main prey. Nest is often built in the crown of a *Euphorbia*.

Length: 75 cm  ss: immature Bateleur (see below)

## Bateleur

Stocky, mostly black eagle with **scarlet face and legs**. The back and tail are chestnut. In flight, the female can be told from the male by the much thinner black line on the trailing edge of the **white wings**. Immature is plain brown with **dark eyes** (Brown Snake Eagle has yellow eyes). Flies as though balancing on a tightrope; feet protruding beyond the **extremely short tail**. Feeds on small animals and carrion. Nests below canopy of a tree.

Length: 60 cm

## Yellowbilled Kite

Dark brown raptor with long dexterous wings. The **broad triangular tail**, often held in a V-shape, is diagnostic. The legs, cere and bill of the adult are yellow. The immature has a black bill, as does the similar **Black Kite** – which can be told apart by its grey head. Often scavenges, so is frequently seen along roads and villages. Nests below the canopy of a leafy tree. **Summer migrant**.
Length: 56 cm  ss: Steppe Buzzard (45-50 cm)

EF  RF  B  G

## Gymnogene

Large, pale grey raptor with broad wings and small head. The **bare face** is yellow, but becomes pink when excited. The underparts are finely barred. In flight, the **black tail, with a single, broad white band**, is diagnostic. The immature is brown and buff, and can be confused with other raptors. The long yellow legs are double-jointed and used to extract prey from holes. Nests in a tall tree.
Length: 65 cm  ss: Dark Chanting Goshawk

EF  RO  B  T

## Blackshouldered Kite

Small, pale grey raptor with snow-white head and underparts and diagnostic **black shoulder patches**. The feet and cere are yellow and the eyes bright red. The immature is blotched in ash-brown and white. Often perches on the highest available point and typically wags its tail. Regularly hovers above grassland. Rodents are the main prey. The nest is built within a shrub or tree.
Length: 33 cm

EF  G

## Lizard Buzzard

Small stocky raptor with pale grey head and upperparts and white underbelly barred in grey. The **throat is white with a diagnostic black stripe** down the middle; feet and cere are red. Immature paler than adult. The back of the black tail has a single, broad white band (rarely two). Usually perches on the outer branches of a tree and may draw attention to itself with its melodious whistled call.
Length: 36 cm  ss: Gabar Goshawk (32 cm, no white bar on tail, no black stripe on throat)

LEX HES

EF  T  B

49

## Steppe Buzzard

Medium-sized raptor mottled in brown and fawn, with a **smudgy pale bar on the breast**. The cere and legs are yellow. Much variation in plumage occurs. In flight the **dark tips of the feathers and pale wing panels** are noticeable. **Summer visitor.** Preys mostly on rodents. Uncommon in the Lowveld proper, but the most abundant large raptor in summer in the escarpment foothills.
Length: 45 to 50 cm

## Dark Chanting Goshawk

Large, dark grey hawk with **long red legs and feet**. The pale underbelly is finely barred. Usually perches in an erect posture on open branches or telephone poles along roadsides. Immature is ashy-brown above with cream underbelly barred in rufous; the long legs and erect posture distinguish it from other immature hawks. Feeds on lizards, snakes, large insects, birds and rodents. Call is a flute-like wail.
Length: 50 to 56 cm

## African Goshawk

Medium-sized hawk with pale grey head and upperparts and white underparts barred in rufous up to the throat. The legs and eyes are yellow and the **cere is grey**. The female is considerably larger than the male. Keeps to dense cover but may draw attention to itself by its distinctive 'chip' call uttered at rest or in display flights. Lacks the white rump of the smaller Little Sparrowhawk.
Length: 36 to 40 cm  ss: Little Sparrowhawk (24 cm)

## Secretarybird

Large terrestrial raptor with long legs and quill-like plumes protruding from the back of the head. The bare face is orange and the legs are pink. Occurs in pairs in open country where it searches for snakes, lizards and rodents. Runs along ground before taking flight. A pair of elongated tail feathers extend past the tail to provide a distinctive flight outline. Nests on top of a low tree.
Length: 1.4 m

50

## Cape Turtle Dove

Medium-sized, pale grey dove with black neck collar finely edged in white. The **black eyes and pale grey breast** distinguish it from the next species. The evocative 'kuk-cooo-kuk' call is one of Africa's typical sounds. Usually found in pairs, but may gather in large flocks at water in the dry season. Small twig nest is built within a shrub or tree. Seeds are the main diet.

Length: 28 cm

EF B G

## Redeyed Dove

Large, **pink-headed** dove with bold black collar. The breast is rosy-pink and the **red eyes** are surrounded by red skin. The similar Mourning Dove is smaller with a pale grey head and pale yellow eyes. Keeps to dense vegetation but may venture onto lawns in gardens and restcamps. The typical call is a drawn-out 'coooo' but the nasal alarm – **'njeeh'** – is distinctive. Nest and diet as per the next species.

Length: 35 cm  ss: Mourning Dove (30 cm)

EF RF

## Mourning Dove

Large, **grey-headed** dove with bold black collar. The breast is pinkish, and the **pale yellow eyes** are surrounded by bare red skin. The similar Redeyed Dove is larger, with a pale pink head and red eyes. Common in KNP restcamps from Satara northwards. The soft **'kook-kurrrr'** call gives this bird its name. The small twig nest is often built in a thorn tree. Feeds on seeds.

Length: 30 cm  ss: Redeyed Dove (35 cm)

T RF

## Laughing Dove

Small, brick-red and grey dove with pink head and ʰreast **speckled in black**. Common and widespread in the more open habitats and, like other doves, dependent upon drinking water. Most often found in pairs but may form flocks at waterholes. The call is a soft cooing, often uttered at midday. Abundant and tame in camps and gardens. Feeds mostly on seeds. The nest is a small twig structure.

Length: 26 cm

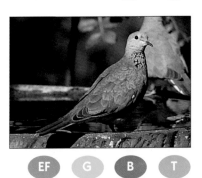

EF G B T

## Greenspotted Dove

Small, cinnamon-brown dove with pale forehead. Four or five **emerald-green spots** are displayed on the closed wing. In flight, the **chestnut wings** are distinctive. The descending call – 'doo-doo-du-du-dududu' – is one of Africa's most evocative sounds. Shyer than other doves, but frequently seen on quiet sand roads. The twig nest is often built in an exposed site. Seeds are the main food.
Length: 22 cm  ss: Tambourine Dove (white below)

## Namaqua Dove

Small dove with distinctive long tail. The male has a **black mask and throat**, and **yellow bill** with a red base; female has a uniform grey head and throat. Both sexes have small, indigo-blue wing-spots. In flight, the **chestnut wings** are distinctive. Occurs in pairs or small flocks in sparsely vegetated areas. Nomadic, with numbers fluctuating in relation to rainfall. The call is a double-note hoot.
Length: 28 cm

## African Green Pigeon

Parrot-like dove with olive-green back, grey-green head and yellow leggings. The eye is pale mauve, the base of the bill and feet red, and the leggings are bright yellow. Feeds mostly on figs. Small flocks are often seen flying in and out of large trees. Frail twig nests are built in tall trees. The call is a series of clicking notes followed by a jumble of liquid whistles.
Length: 30 cm

MARK TENNANT/AFRICAN IMAGES

## Doublebanded Sandgrouse

Pigeon-like bird with **pointed wings**. The male is speckled on the back with a sandy breast rimmed with two bars in black and white. The eye is surrounded by bare yellow skin, and the forehead is black and white. Females are cryptically coloured. Usually in pairs, but flocks gather to drink at dusk. Most often seen on the verges of sand roads. Camouflaged eggs are laid on the ground.
Length: 25 cm

## Grey Lourie

Large, ashy-grey bird with a distinctive **crest of lacy feathers and a long tail**. Occurs in pairs during the breeding season, but flocks may gather around waterholes in the dry winter months. Most common in dry savanna, but never far from water. The call is a nasal 'gweeeh' ('go away') – often uttered in alarm. Feeds mostly on berries and leaf buds. The nest is a bowl of twigs set in a thorn tree.
Length: 48 cm

BETH PETERSON/AFRICAN IMAGES

## Purplecrested Lourie

Large, multi-coloured bird with blue-green back and tail, cinnamon breast and **iridescent purple crest**. In flight the spectacular **crimson wings** are obvious. Occurs in pairs or troops of up to a dozen. Bounds along branches of large trees, feeding on figs and fruit. The call is a harsh 'kok-kok-kok'. Usually rather shy but may visit garden bird baths. The nest is a small bowl of twigs.
Length: 46 cm

## Brownheaded Parrot

Small green parrot with a brown head. The **underwings and vent are luminous yellow**. Occurs in pairs or small flocks which draw attention to themselves by their shrill piercing calls. Feeds on figs, fruit and the seeds of trees such as *Acacia* and *Terminalia*. Drinks regularly and is often seen at waterholes. Nests in a hole, usually in a dead tree.
Length: 24 cm  ss: Cape Parrot (35 cm; only occurs in the far north of the KNP)

## Diederik Cuckoo

Small, coppery-green cuckoo with snow-white underparts. The male is **metallic green** above, with **red eyes** ringed by red skin. The female is bronze above, spotted in buff. The immature has an orange bill. A **summer migrant** from central Africa. Its name is derived from the repetitive call –'di-di-deederik'. Eggs are laid in the nests of sparrows, weavers and bishops.
Length: 18 cm  ss: Klaas's Cuckoo (18 cm)

RF · EF · T

## Redchested Cuckoo

Pale-grey bird with long pointed wings. The **chest is rusty-red** and the underparts buffy with grey bars. Young birds are darker. Elusive **summer migrant**. The repetitive 'piet-my-vrou' call of the male is a familiar sound in midsummer, sometimes carrying on into the night. The female's call is a shrill 'pipi-pipipi'. Lays its eggs in the nests of other birds, particularly the various robins.

Length: 30 cm  ss: African Cuckoo; Black Cuckoo

RW · RF

## Burchell's Coucal

Large, chestnut-red bird with black head and creamy-white underparts. Flies on broad wings in a floppy, unbalanced manner. In early mornings and evenings, it utters its bubbling call which sounds like liquid being poured from a bottle. Sometimes ventures onto lawns. Feeds on large insects, rodents and nestling birds. Related to the cuckoos, but it rears its own young.

Length: 44 cm

G · B · T

## Pearlspotted Owl

Tiny rufous owl with white spots on the head and back. The breast is white with rufous streaking; the yellow eyes framed with broad white brows. The longish tail is often wagged up and down. This little owl is active by day and night. The call is a whistle, rising to a crescendo and ending in drawn-out notes. Insects are the main prey. Nests in a tree hole. Larger **Barred Owl** has a barred breast.

Length: 18 cm  ss: Barred Owl (21 cm)

T · B · G

## Scops Owl

Tiny, cryptically plumaged owl with ear tufts and yellow eyes. The back is blotched and the breast streaked. Roosts by day against the trunk of a tree – Knobthorn and Mopane are favoured – where it is superbly camouflaged. The repetitive 'pruuup' call is one of Africa's most evocative night sounds. Feeds primarily on insects. Eggs are laid in a tree hole. Larger **Whitefaced Owl** has orange eyes.

Length: 20 cm  ss: Whitefaced Owl (28 cm)

## Spotted Eagle Owl

Large, grey-brown owl with dark blotches on the back and fine barring on the breast. The **ear-tufts** are distinctive and the **eyes are bright yellow**. Nocturnal, but frequently seen in suburbs where it hunts under lights. Sits on roads, often with dire consequences. Breeds in holes in trees or among rocks. Feeds on a variety of small creatures, including winged termites. The call is a low, deep 'whoooo'.
Length: 45 cm

## Giant Eagle Owl

Huge, grey-brown owl with pale face rimmed in black, and diagnostic **pink eyelids** above black eyes. The ear-tufts create a cat-like silhouette. Young birds are paler with fine barring. Occurs in pairs, often along watercourses. Eggs are normally laid in an abandoned eagle nest. Smaller mammals and birds up to the size of Helmeted Guineafowl are the prey. Call is a deep 'ooomph' grunt.
Length: 65 cm

## Wood Owl

Medium-sized, rufous-brown owl with dark eyes set in a pale face; there are **no ear-tufts**. The underparts are creamy-white with bold barring. The **bill is pale yellow**. Occurs in pairs in dense vegetation along larger rivers and in wooded valleys in the escarpment foothills. The lovely hooting call is often described as 'who, who, who are you'. Nests in a tree hole. Prey includes rodents and insects.
Length: 35 cm  ss: Marsh Owl (open grasslands)

## Fierynecked Nightjar

Nocturnal bird with cryptic, brown and fawn plumage. Rarely seen, and known mostly by its beautiful call – often described as 'good Lord, deliver us'. Most vociferous during the dry season, and particularly on moonlit nights. **Roosts and perches on branches**, seldom alighting on the ground. Moths and other insects are captured on the wing.
Length: 24 cm  ss: Mozambique Nightjar; Freckled Nightjar; European Nightjar

LEX HES

55

BRENDAN RYAN

# Redfaced Mousebird

Small, pale grey, mouse-like bird with a long tail. The underparts are buffy. The **bright red facial skin** is diagnostic. Occurs in small flocks which usually fly together, and speedily, from one place to the next. Birds huddle together at their roost. Soft fruit and berries are the main food. A small stick nest is built within a tangled bush or creeper. Call is a clear whistle.
Length: 34 cm

# Speckled Mousebird

Small, dark grey, mouse-like bird with a very long tail. The underbelly is buffy. The face is black and the **lower bill white**. Unlike the Redfaced Mousebird, flocks **usually fly singly**, in a panicky fashion, from bush to bush. Birds huddle together when roosting. Favours tangled growth in which to roost and breed. Berries and soft fruit make up the bulk of their diet. Call is a harsh chatter.
Length: 35 cm

# Palm Swift

Ash-brown swift differing from all martins and swallows in its more rapid flight, and **long, sickle-shaped wings**. The long tail is deeply forked. Often seen skimming the surface of water at dusk. Occurs in small flocks wherever Lala Palms grow, and around ornamental palm trees in towns. The nest is affixed to palm fronds, and the eggs are secured with a sticky secretion.
Length: 17 cm

# Whiterumped Swift

Black swift with a **deeply-forked tail** often held closed in flight. The **white rump** is conspicuous from above. In common with all swifts, it spends most of its time on the wing, hawking for tiny insects, and is physically unable to perch on wires or branches. Compared to swallows, the **wings are long and pointed to create a sickle-shaped outline**. Nests in old swallow nests. Absent in midwinter.
Length: 15 cm  ss: Little Swift (square tail)

## Wiretailed Swallow

Blue-black swallow with **orange cap** and snow-white underparts. The wire-like tail streamers are so thin as to be almost invisible. Occurs in pairs or small groups, invariably near water. Feeds on the wing, taking small insects such as gnats and flies. Call is an excited 'chisik-chisik'. Mud pellet nest is built under bridges, verandas or under the branches of trees overhanging water.
Length: 13 cm

## European Swallow

Blue-black swallow with chestnut fore-head and throat, **broad black collar** and cream underparts. Immature is dusky. Gregarious, non-breeding **summer migrant** from Europe. Flocks of up to 200 hawk flying insects in open habitats. Night-time roosts in reedbeds may host thousands of birds. Prior to heading north in March-April, large numbers assemble on trees and overhead wires.
Length: 18 cm  ss: Greyrumped Swallow

## Lesser Striped Swallow

Blue-black swallow with **orange head and face**, and pale breast lined with bold black streaks. Occurs in pairs or small flocks, usually near water. Feeds on the wing, taking small insects such as gnats and flies. Call is a series of nasal mew-ing notes. Mud pellet nest is built under bridges, eaves or under the branches of trees. May become tame and confiding. **Summer migrant** from central Africa.
Length: 16 cm  ss: Greater Striped Swallow (20 cm)

## Redbreasted Swallow

Large, blue-black swallow with brick-red underparts. The **underwing coverts are buffy**. Occurs in pairs, usually in the immediate vicinity of their mud pellet nests which are commonly built under road culverts. **Summer migrant** from central Africa. More common in the southern Lowveld. The similar **Mosque Swallow** has a white throat and white underwing coverts.
Length: 24 cm  ss: Mosque Swallow (24 cm)

57

## Giant Kingfisher

Massive, charcoal-grey kingfisher with a white-spotted back. Sexes differ in that the **male has only the breast rufous**, while the **female is rufous on the underbelly and underwings**. Feeds mostly on crabs, but also takes fish and frogs. Fishes alone or in pairs. The loud 'khak-khak-khak' call is often made in flight. The nest is a tunnel excavated in a steep river bank or termite mound.
Length: 46 cm

## Pied Kingfisher

Medium-sized, black and white kingfisher. The white underparts are divided by a **double chest bar in the male**, and a **single broken bar in the female**. Hunts for fish by hovering above water and plunging in after prey. Occurs in pairs or family groups, and nests in a sandbank burrow. Most frequently seen kingfisher in the region and often shows little fear of people. Call is a series of twitters.
Length: 28 cm

## Malachite Kingfisher

Tiny, jewel-like kingfisher with bright blue back, orange underparts and **scarlet bill**. The crest is the colour of malachite stone, banded in black. Sexes are alike. Immature has a black bill. Perches among reeds and sedges. Fish, frogs, tadpoles and aquatic insects are the prey. Call is a high-pitched whistle. Nests in a burrow in a sandbank. Similar **Pygmy Kingfisher** has violet cheeks and orange eyebrows.
Length: 14 cm  ss: Pygmy Kingfisher (13 cm)

## Striped Kingfisher

Small, dark-backed kingfisher with blue wings and tail. A **black stripe runs through the eye**, the pale chest is streaked and the bill is dull red. Favours open woodland, where it hunts for insects and small lizards. The eggs are laid in an abandoned woodpecker hole in summer. Call is a repetitive 'chee-cherrrr', most often made at dusk and frequently accompanied by open wing displays.
Length: 18 cm

## Woodland Kingfisher

Medium-sized, turquoise-blue kingfisher with **black shoulders** and **red and black bill**. Immature is duller with shorter, reddish-brown bill. Like the next species, this kingfisher does not fish, but feeds on large insects and lizards. Favours open areas with tall trees, breeding in wood-pecker or barbet holes. A **summer migrant** from central Africa. Call is a piercing, repetitive trill – 'tri-tri-trirrrrrrrr'.
Length: 23 cm: Greyhooded Kingfisher (20 cm)

## Brownhooded Kingfisher

Medium-sized kingfisher with long, dusky-red bill and **turquoise-blue wings**. The back of the male is black, that of the female brown. Occurs singly or in pairs **away from water**, preying on large insects and lizards. Perches conspicuously and calls with a sharp, descending whistle, or a harsh 'klee-klee-klee' alarm. Eggs are laid in a self-excavated hole in an earth bank.
Length: 24 cm  ss: Greyhooded Kingfisher (20 cm)

## Lilacbreasted Roller

Brilliantly coloured roller with **electric blue wings and tail** – most distinctive in flight. The breast and cheeks are lilac. Streamers protrude beyond the tail. Occurs in pairs in open areas, perching conspicuously on dead trees and termite mounds. Summer courtship display involves aerial rolls and tumbles. Eggs are laid in a tree hole nest. Prey includes large insects and lizards.
Length: 36 cm  ss: Rackettailed Roller (north only)

## European Roller

Pale blue roller with rufous back and bright blue wings. The **tail lacks streamers**. A **migrant** from the Mediterranean present between December and March when it may outnumber the previous species. Feeds on insects. The larger **Purple Roller** has blue on the wings and tail only, the smaller **Broadbilled Roller** has a bright yellow bill.
Length: 31 cm  ss: Purple Roller; Broadbilled Roller

59

## Little Bee-eater

Small, green-backed bee-eater with fawn underparts and yellow throat with black collar. A thin blue eyebrow is present. The **square tail** is green and buff with a black tip. Occurs in pairs or family groups in open woodland and on flood-plains. Hawks butterflies and other flying insects from low perches. Nests in a burrow in an earth bank or termite mound. Call is a soft tinkling note.
Length: 18 cm

## Carmine Bee-eater

Large, bright pink bee-eater with turquoise cap, and blue rump and vent. Like all bee-eaters, a black mask runs through the eye. Young birds are dull pink and lack the long tail streamers of adults. Soars with pointed wings, snapping up bees and other insects. Gregarious, non-breeding **summer migrant** most common between December and March. Call is a rolling 'trrerrk-trrerrk'.
Length: 36 cm

## Whitefronted Bee-eater

Medium-sized, green-backed bee-eater. The **throat is red**, forehead white and **vent bright blue**. A white band runs below the black mask. The **square tail lacks streamers**. Immatures are duller. Prefers well-wooded areas, usually near water. Breeds in colonies of up to 20 pairs in sandbank burrows, sometimes alongside kingfishers. Flying insects are the prey. Call is a nasal 'squerr'.
Length: 24 cm

## European Bee-eater

Large, **golden-backed** bee-eater with turquoise wings, tail and underparts. The yellow throat is fringed with a black collar. A pair of streamers protrudes beyond the tail of the adult. The immature is duller. Non-breeding **summer migrant** from the Mediterranean. Occurs in flocks of up to 100 in open habitats. Feeds mostly on bees but, like other bee-eaters, swarms around grass fires to snap up fleeing grasshoppers. The call is a liquid 'prrrup'.
Length: 28 cm   ss: Bluecheeked Bee-eater

## Yellowbilled Hornbill

Medium-sized, black and white hornbill with distinctive **yellow bill**. The bare skin around the pale yellow eyes is red, as is the throat patch. Favours open, dry habitats, spending much time on the ground in search of beetles. Nests in a tree cavity, with the female enclosing herself with the eggs. The hollow call – 'toka-toka-toka' – is made with the head lowered and wings raised.
Length: 55 cm

## Redbilled Hornbill

Small, black and white hornbill with distinctive **red bill**. There is no bare skin on the face. Favours broad-leaved woodland, especially mature Mopane, but may occur alongside the Yellowbilled Hornbill. Spends much time on the ground in search of beetles. Nests in a tree hole, with the female enclosing herself with the eggs. The call is a series of clucking notes.
Length: 46 cm  ss: Crowned Hornbill (54 cm)

## Grey Hornbill

Small, grey and white hornbill with a bold **white eye-stripe**. The bill of the male is black with a yellow panel and a small casque, while that of the female is horn-coloured with a maroon tip. Occurs in pairs when breeding but may form small flocks during the dry season. Insects and berries make up the bulk of the diet. The dipping flight and plaintive whistled call are distinctive.
Length: 46 cm

## Trumpeter Hornbill

Large black hornbill with white underbelly and trailing edge to the secondary flight feathers. The massive bill is topped by a hollow casque – much larger in the male. Occurs in pairs, or troops of twenty or more which fly lazily from one fruiting tree to another; figs are the favoured food. The call is a drawn-out wail, not unlike the cry of a human baby. Breeds in a tree hole.
Length: 58 cm

MARK TENNANT/AFRICAN IMAGES

## Ground Hornbill

Huge black hornbill with massive bill. Bare skin around the eyes and throat of the adult is red; the female has a blue patch on the throat. The immature has pale yellow facial skin. When airborne, the white flight feathers are conspicuous. Lives in family groups of up to seven which walk along in search of prey such as tortoises and snakes. The call is a deep 'oooom'. Nests in a large tree hole.
Length: 90 cm

BRENDAN RYAN

## Redbilled Woodhoopoe

Long-tailed, ink-blue bird with a metallic green sheen. The long **curved bill and short legs are coral-red**. An active and noisy bird which lives in family groups of five or more. The cackling call is made in unison and often culminates with all the birds rocking back and forth on branches. Insect larvae are extracted from under the bark of trees. Young are reared in a tree hole.
Length: 36 cm  ss: Greater Scimitarbill (26 cm)

## Hoopoe

Distinctive, brick-red bird with black and white wings and a fan-shaped crest. The long curved bill is used for probing the ground for worms and insects. In flight it resembles a giant butterfly. Usually seen singly or in pairs, less often in family groups; favours dryer open areas. Nests in a cavity in a tree, often quite low to the ground. The call is a repetitive 'hoop-hoop-hoop'.
Length: 28 cm

## Crested Barbet

Multi-coloured barbet with **yellow and red underparts and face**, and black back blotched in white. The stout **pale bill** is used to excavate nest holes in the branches of trees. The ragged crest is raised when the 'alarm clock trill' call is made. Occurs in pairs in dryer, more open habitats. Fruit and berries are the favoured food, but ground-dwelling insects are also eaten.
Length: 23 cm

62

## Blackcollared Barbet

Stocky barbet with **crimson-red face** bordered by a **black collar**. The back is olive-green and the underparts buffy-yellow. The stout **black bill** is used to excavate nest holes in the branches of trees. Noisy and conspicuous, it occurs in pairs or family groups. The call is a repetitive 'duduloo-duduloo' in duet or chorus. Insects, berries and fruit – especially figs – are the favoured food.

Length: 20 cm  ss: Acacia Pied Barbet (18 cm)

EF  T  RF

## Yellowfronted Tinker Barbet

Tiny barbet with black upperparts flecked in white, and pale yellow underparts. A bright yellow (or orange) spot is present on the forehead. Rather inconspicuous, but noticeable due to its monotonous 'pop-pop-pop-pop-pop' call – made with hardly a pause on warm days. Feeds on small berries, especially those of tree parasites such as *Tapinanthus*. Eggs are laid in a small, self-excavated tree hole.

Length: 23 cm  ss: Goldenrumped Tinker Barbet

LEX HES

EF

## Bearded Woodpecker

Large, olive-backed woodpecker with **pale grey underparts barred in white**. The male has a scarlet crown and finely spotted forehead; the female has no red on the head. The white face has broad black streaks behind the eye and below the bill. Usually seen in pairs in the branches of taller trees. The call is a rapid 'wik-wik-wik' or a resonant drumming. Eggs are laid in a self-made tree hole.

Length: 26 cm  ss: Bennett's Woodpecker (24 cm)

B  T

## Cardinal Woodpecker

Small, olive-backed woodpecker with **white underparts streaked in brown**. The male has a scarlet crown while that of the female is black. Both sexes have a diagnostic **plain brown forehead**, and a single dark streak running from the base of the bill. Occurs in pairs, often in mixed bird parties. Nests in a self-made tree hole. Call is series of 'kree-kree' notes. Insect larvae are the main food.

Length: 15 cm  ss: Goldentailed Woodpecker (23 cm)

EF  T  B

63

## Sabota Lark

Small, rufous-brown bird with distinctive **white eye-stripe** and throat. The back is blotched and the pale breast streaked in brown. Occurs singly or in pairs along roadsides, frequently **perching in low bushes** to deliver its song. Feeds on insects. Most abundant in the central KNP. The similar **Monotonous Lark** has no eye-stripe; the **Bushveld Pipit** has white outer tail feathers.

Length: 15 cm  ss: Monotonous Lark; Bushveld Pipit

JOHN CARLYON

## Greater Honeyguide

Drab, brown and buff bird with distinctive **white outer tail feathers** most obvious in **dipping flight**. Male has a pale pink bill, black throat and white ear-patch. Immature has a dark back and pale yellow underparts. May guide people to bee-hives, and feeds on bee larvae and wax. Male calls 'whit-purr' monotonously from a territorial tree-top perch. Calls mostly during summer.

Length: 20 cm  ss: Lesser Honeyguide (15 cm)

## Blackeyed Bulbul

Lively bulbul with brown back, pale underparts and distinctive **yellow vent**. The black head has a small crest which gives a peaked appearance. Occurs in pairs or family groups in well-wooded areas. Confiding and often common in gardens and camps. The call is a series of liquid whistles, but the 'cheet-cheet-cheet' alarm call is better known. Small insects and berries are eaten.

Length: 22 cm

BRENDAN RYAN

## Sombre Bulbul

Drab, olive-brown bulbul with no distinguishing features other than its **white eyes**. Secretive, it usually keeps to dense cover but may be seen feeding on figs and fruit on exposed branches. Occurs singly or in pairs but is more often heard than seen. The call – described by some as: 'Willie – come out and fight – scaaaaared' – is usually uttered from the top of a leafy tree.

Length: 14 cm  ss: Terrestrial Bulbul (brown eyes)

## Groundscraper Thrush

Grey-backed thrush with **white underparts boldly streaked in black**. The face is white with distinctive black stripes behind the eyes. In flight, the **buffy wing panels** are distinctive. Immature has scaly appearance to the back, and less obvious streaking. Occurs in pairs in open areas where it feeds on insects. Stands in an **upright posture**. The call is a sequence of whistled notes.
Length: 22 cm  ss: Dusky Lark (19 cm)

## Kurrichane Thrush

Grey-brown thrush with **orange bill** and orange-buff underparts. The faintly speckled white throat has a pair of black, moustache-like streaks. Immature is paler, mottled and streaked in buff. Spends most of the time on the ground, searching through leaves for insects and worms. Often feeds on lawns around camps and lodges. Call is a clear 'tseeeou' whistle.
Length: 22 cm

## Arrowmarked Babbler

Drab brown bird with bright orange eyes and **bold white streaks – in the shape of arrows – on the crown, throat and chest**. Immature lacks white streaks and is paler overall. Favours tangled vegetation and is less often seen than heard. Gregarious and noisy; the call is a raucous cackle – not unlike that of the Redbilled Woodhoopoe – uttered in unison by groups of up to 12 birds.
Length: 24 cm

## Whitebrowed Scrub Robin

Small brown robin with white **underparts heavily streaked** in dark brown. The bold white eye-stripes and white wing bars are distinctive. The long tail is chestnut at the base, merging to black and tipped in white; it is raised up and down to reveal the white vent. Avoids dense woodland, preferring open scrub with acacia. Call is a flutey whistle, made mostly at dawn and dusk.
Length: 15 cm  ss: Eastern Bearded Robin (18 cm)

JOHN CARLYON

RF  EF

## Heuglin's Robin

**Bright orange** robin with slate-grey back. The black head is divided by a **bold white eye-stripe**. Immature is heavily speckled. Occurs in pairs. May become confiding in gardens and restcamps, but is otherwise secretive. Extremely vociferous – the strident dawn and dusk call is a series of clear whistled notes; a churring alarm may also be uttered. Feeds on insects caught among leaf litter.
Length: 20 cm  ss: Whitethroated Robin (17 cm)

RF  EF

## Natal Robin

**Bright orange** robin with **blue-grey back**. The crown is reddish. Immature is heavily mottled. Occurs in pairs in dense habitats, most common south of the Sabie River. May become confiding in gardens and restcamps, but is otherwise secretive. The usual call is a soft 'tree-troou', but a wide repertoire of liquid songs, including those of other birds, is also given. Most active at dusk and dawn. Feeds on insects.
Length: 18 cm

EF  RW

## Stone Chat

Small chubby chat. Male is boldly marked with chocolate back, black head, **white neck collar** and chestnut breast. Female is mottled on the back with grey head, and fawn breast and underparts. Both have distinctive **white rump and wing bars** in flight. Perches conspicuously in low vegetation or on edges of reedbeds, coming to ground for insects. Solitary or in pairs. Call is a grating 'tsik-tsik'.
Length: 14 cm

RO

## Mocking Chat

Dark chat restricted to rocky habitats. The male is blue-black on the head, back and wings, with a **bright chestnut rump and belly**. The white shoulder patch is variable in size. The female is charcoal-grey on the back with rusty underparts. As its name suggests, it is an accomplished mimic of other birds' songs. Usually lays its eggs in the mud-cup nest of a swallow, first breaking away the entrance tunnel.
Length: 23 cm

# African Pied Wagtail

Small, black and white bird with a **long tail** which is constantly bobbed up and down. Immature is a dull version of the adult. Occurs in pairs or family groups along rivers and is often seen foraging on lawns of restcamps and gardens. Small insects and worms are the main food. The nest is built in a crack in a rock or under the eaves of a building. The call is a strident whistle.

Length: 20 cm  ss: Cape Wagtail (19 cm)

# Southern Black Tit

Small black bird with **white shoulder patches** and **white edges to the wing feathers**. The female is dusky-grey rather than black. Differs from the previous species with its longer tail, black head and restless behaviour. Pairs or small groups clamber through tangled vegetation and hang from bark in search of insects. Call is a harsh 'cherr-cherr-cherr'. Often found in mixed bird parties.

Length: 16 cm  ss: Arnot's Chat (Mopane woodland)

# Forktailed Drongo

Glossy black bird with **deeply forked tail**. Females are greyish below. The **red eyes** are diagnostic. The **hooked bill** has long bristles at its base. In flight, the **wings are noticeably paler than the body**. Occurs singly or in pairs in most habitats. Hawks insects from an exposed perch, often alongside large mammals. Call is a jumble of grating metallic notes. It frequently mobs eagles and hawks.

Length: 25 cm

LEX HES

# Black Flycatcher

Glossy black bird with **square or slightly notched tail**. The eyes are dark brown. When perched, the **brown edges to the wing feathers** can be seen. The bill is not strongly hooked. Occurs singly or in pairs in well-wooded habitats. Insects are hawked from an exposed perch but usually captured on the ground. Call is a soft twitter. Unobtrusive, but confiding and often seen around camps and lodges.

Length: 19 cm  ss: Black Cuckooshrike (22 cm)

67

## Paradise Flycatcher

Small, **chestnut-backed** bird with indigo-blue head and smoky-grey underparts merging to white vent. The bill and eye wattles are turquoise-blue. Breeding male differs from female in extravagant, **ribbon-like tail**. Occurs in pairs. Tiny, egg-cup nest is often conspicuous at the tip of a branch. Call is a gentle 'wee-we-diddly' or a 'jweet' alarm. **Summer migrant**, but some may overwinter.

Length: 23 cm (plus 18 cm tail in breeding male)

RF   EF

## Bluegrey Flycatcher

Small, **blue-grey bird with dark eyes ringed in white**, pale underside and white vent. Occurs in pairs or small family groups. Often confiding, it hawks insects in the air, or captures them on the ground, in close proximity to people. The call is soft sibilant whistle. Nest is a small cup, bound with spiderwebs. Most active at dusk. The similar **Fantailed Flycatcher** has a black tail edged in white.

Length: 15 cm  ss: Fantailed Flycatcher (14 cm)

EF   RF

## Spotted Flycatcher

Small, pale brown bird with off-white underparts. The name is misleading, as the **breast and forehead are finely streaked**, not spotted. Typically perches low down on the outermost branches of a tree or shrub, launching out to catch flying insects. **Flicks wings on alighting**. Solitary, quiet and inconspicuous. Non-breeding **summer migrant** from Europe.

Length: 14 cm  ss: Dusky Flycatcher (12 cm);
Mousecoloured Flycatcher (17 cm, plain breast)

T   B   EF

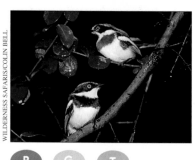

WILDERNESS SAFARIS/COLIN BELL

## Chinspot Batis

Tiny, black and white bird with grey crown and mantle. **Bright yellow eyes are set in a black mask**. The male has a broad black bar on the breast, the female a chestnut breast bar and spot on the throat. Immature is mottled. Usually seen in pairs, moving methodically through branches in search of insects. Call is a whistled 'di-di-deee' ('three blind mice'), or a harsh alarm.

Length: 13 cm  ss: Wattle-eyed Flycatcher (18 cm)

B   G   T

# Blackbacked Puffback

Small, black-backed shrike with snow-white underparts and white edging to the wing feathers. The eyes are **bright red**. Displaying males erect a puffy mass of white feathers over their back. Female is duller, with a pale face. Noisy, restless and often confiding. In pairs or mixed bird parties in dense foliage. Feeds on small insects. One of the calls from its repertoire is a sharp 'tjick-wheeou'.

Length: 18 cm  ss: Brubru (15 cm, chestnut flanks)

BRENDAN RYAN

# White Helmetshrike

Medium-sized, black-backed shrike with white underparts and wing bar. The pale grey head is fringed with short, forward-facing plumes. The yellow eyes are ringed by **yellow eye wattles**. Gregarious. Restless flocks of up to 12 fly from tree to tree. Call is a muffled 'chiroo' – often made in chorus by the group. Feeds on insects. **Redbilled Helmetshrike** is black with white vent, red bill and eyes.

Length: 20 cm  ss: Redbilled Helmetshrike (22 cm)

# Whitecrowned Shrike

Large, ash-brown shrike with **white crown** and underparts. A dark line runs through the eye to form a **collar on the nape**. Gregarious; small flocks of up to ten perch erect on outer branches of trees, dropping to the ground to capture beetles, other insects and caterpillars. Call is a thin whistle or harsh chatter. Neat, spiderweb-bound nest is often built on an exposed branch.

Length: 25 cm  ss: Lesser Grey Shrike (21 cm)

# Longtailed Shrike

Large, all-black shrike with **long tail**, and white wing bar and tips of the wing feathers. Female is duller, with a shorter tail and white flanks. Gregarious, small flocks of up to ten perch conspicuously in woodland or open areas. Beetles, grasshoppers and other insects are caught on the ground. Call is a squeaky whistle – 'pruuit-preeuo'. Groups are prone to local movements.

Length: 40 to 50 cm

LEX HES

## Southern Boubou

Black and white shrike with **buffy underparts**. Female is more buffy below. With a **white V-pattern on the back** it is superficially similar to the Fiscal Shrike. The body is held in a horizontal, rather than upright, posture. Occurs in pairs which keep mostly to the interior of low shrubs and dense foliage. The **calls are varied**, including liquid or grating notes usually uttered in duet.
Length: 23 cm  ss: Tropical Boubou (far north)

## Fiscal Shrike

Black and white shrike with **long tail** and **white V-pattern on the back**. Females have a rust wash on their flanks. Young are mottled and barred in brown and white. Perches conspicuously, in **upright posture**. Feeds mostly on large insects, spearing victims onto thorns or barbed wire. Uncommon in the KNP but abundant in agricultural lands and along roads in rural areas.
Length: 23 cm  ss: Lesser Grey Shrike (21 cm)

## Redbacked Shrike

Small shrike with sexes not alike. The male has a rich **chestnut back**, pale grey head and rump, white underparts and **black mask**. The female is duller on the back, lacks the black mask and is barred on the underparts. Occurs singly in open habitats, perching low on outer branches. Insects are taken on the ground. Silent. Non-breeding **summer migrant**.
Length: 18 cm ss: Threestreaked Tchagra (19 cm); Blackcrowned Tchagra  (23 cm)

## Redbilled Oxpecker

Dull brown bird with buffy underparts and **bright red bill**. The **red eyes are ringed with bare yellow skin**. Immature has dark eyes and bill. Gregarious – groups of five or more ride on the backs of large mammals, gathering ticks with a scissor motion of the bill. **Giraffe and antelope** are the favoured hosts. Groups sound their rasping call in flight. Nests and roosts in a tree hole.
Length: 22 cm  ss: Yellowbilled Oxpecker

JOHN CARLYON

LEX HES

LEX HES

## Greater Blue-eared Starling

Medium-sized, iridescent, blue-green starling with **pale yellow eyes** and **dark ear-patch** appearing black. Dark wing spots are prominent and the **underbelly is blue**. Occurs in pairs or large noisy flocks. Call is a nasal 'squerr' – similar to that of the Whitefronted Bee-eater. Most abundant and tame in **northern KNP** restcamps where it outnumbers the next species. Breeds in a tree hole.

Length: 23 cm  ss: Glossy Starling

B  T

## Glossy Starling

Medium-sized, iridescent, blue-green starling with **pale yellow eyes**. Not as glossy as the previous species and **lacks dark ear-patches**. The dark wing spots are not prominent and the **underbelly is glossy green**. Occurs in pairs or large noisy flocks. Call is a slurred whistle. Outnumbers the previous species in **southern KNP** restcamps (except at Tshokwane). Breeds in a tree hole.

Length: 23 cm  ss: Blue-eared Glossy Starling

EF  B  T

## Burchell's Starling

Large, glossy, purple-blue starling with **dark eyes** in a dark mask, and long legs. Duller than the previous species. **Long tail is broad and kite-shaped**. Spends much time on the ground in an upright posture,  flying for cover on broad wings. In pairs or small groups, often in the company of hornbills. Beetles and other insects are the main food. Call is a squeaky 'tjerrik'. Breeds in a tree hole.

Length: 34 cm  ss: Longtailed Starling (34 cm)

G  B  T

## Plumcoloured Starling

Small, iridescent, violet-magenta starling with snow-white belly. Female is distinct, with brown upperparts and white under-parts heavily streaked in brown, and yellow gape. Feeds on berries and insects in leafy trees. Occurs in pairs, small groups or flocks of up to 50. Call is a variety of harsh grating notes. **Summer migrant**, breeds in a tree hole. Some individuals may overwinter.

Length: 19 cm

BRENDAN RYAN

EF  RF  B  T

71

## Blackheaded Oriole

Bright, sulphur-yellow bird with greenish back and black head. The **bill and eyes are coral-red**. Immature has a speckled head. Occurs singly or in pairs, often joining mixed bird parties during winter. Insects and caterpillars are caught within the foliage of large trees. Call is a liquid 'pleeoo' whistle, or a harsh nasal alarm. Cup nest is adorned with lichen.

Length: 24 cm  ss: African Golden Oriole (black eye mask); European Golden Oriole (black wings)

## Orangebreasted Bushshrike

Small shrike with **yellow underparts and eyebrow**, grey head and olive-green upperparts; the upper breast is orange. A **black mask** runs through the face. Pairs keep to tangled undergrowth. Call is a strident, up-tempo whistle – 'whi-whi-whi-whi-wheeo' – or a sequence of harsh alarm notes. Feeds on insects. The similar **Gorgeous Bushshrike** has a scarlet throat ringed with a black collar.

Length: 19 cm  ss: Gorgeous Bushshrike (19 cm)

## Greyheaded Bushshrike

Large shrike with yellow underparts, grey head and olive-green upperparts. The **eye is pale yellow**. The **massive bill** is used to tackle prey up to the size of chameleons and small snakes. When in pursuit of prey it may be oblivious to people. Occurs singly or in pairs. The call is a drawn-out 'whooooo' – leading to the alternate name of 'Ghostbird'. The bowl-shaped nest is built in a tall tree.

Length: 26 cm  ss: Orangebreasted Bushshrike

CALLY MAIL

## Goldenbreasted Bunting

Small, golden-yellow finch with chestnut back and wings. The **head is black with two bold white stripes** above and below the eye. White wing bars are conspicuous in flight. Female is paler yellow below. Usually in pairs, but may form small flocks when not breeding. Occurs in well-wooded habitats, where seeds and small insects are the main food. Call is a lively, nasal song.

Length: 16 cm  ss: Rock Bunting (14 cm)

## Spottedbacked Weaver

Medium-sized, yellow weaver. Breeding male has the back boldly spotted in black. The **red eyes** are set in a black mask which extends as an arrow on the chest; the **crown is yellow**. Female and non-breeding male are drab but the **yellow throat contrasts with the whitish belly**. Conspicuous during summer, when activity is centred around large breeding colonies of hanging nests.
Length: 17 cm  ss: Masked Weaver (15 cm)

## Lesser Masked Weaver

Small yellow weaver. Breeding male has **pale yellow eyes** set in a black mask extending to the top of the crown. Female and non-breeding male are drab olive above and uniform pale cream-yellow below; the female has dark eyes. Summer breeding colonies are usually much smaller, and less frenetic, than those of the previous species; hanging nests are often suspended above water.
Length: 15 cm  ss: Masked Weaver (15 cm, red eye)

## Golden Weaver

Medium-sized, yellow weaver with **no mask**, pale eyes and black bill. Back is olive-yellow. Female is slightly duller than the male which does not assume a dull, non-breeding plumage. The woven nest is strung above water, either from a hanging branch or between reeds. Occurs singly or in pairs, sometimes in mixed bird parties. Call is a prolonged swizzle. Insects, berries and seeds are eaten.
Length: 18 cm

## Spectacled Weaver

Small yellow weaver with pale eyes and pointed black bill. The male has a **narrow black mask** and a black stripe extending down the throat, and the face tinged with orange; the female is duller. The woven nest has an extremely long entrance tunnel. Occurs singly or in pairs, often in mixed bird parties; rather shy. Call is a soft, descending whistle. Small insects are the main food.
Length: 16 cm  ss: African Golden Oriole  (24 cm)

73

# Redheaded Weaver

Small weaver. Male in breeding dress has a **scarlet head, orange bill**, dusky-olive tail and wings, and white underbelly. Wing feathers are edged in yellow. Female and non-breeding male differ from other weavers in having an **orange bill**. Occurs in pairs or small groups. Woven **nest incorporates dry leaves** and is suspended from branches or overhead wires. Feeds mostly on insects.
Length: 15 cm

# Red Bishop

Small finch. Male in breeding dress is **crimson with black face and underbelly**. The bill is black. Females and non-breeding males are drab, sparrow-like and easily overlooked. Occurs in reedbeds and floodplains. Displaying male puffs itself into a ball shape and hangs from reed stems. Call is an excited swizzle. Woven nest is built between upright reeds. Feeds on seeds and insects.
Length: 14 cm  ss: Golden Bishop (12 cm)

# Whitewinged Widow

Small finch. Male in breeding dress is pitch black with **white on the wings** and a **small yellow shoulder patch**. The bill is ice-blue; the rounded tail of medium length. Non-breeding male is sparrow-like but retains yellow shoulder; female is drab and nondescript. The related **Redshouldered Widow** has buff on the wings and a red shoulder patch in its male breeding dress.
Length: 19 cm  ss: Redshouldered Widow (19 cm)

# Pintailed Whydah

Tiny finch. Male in breeding dress is black and white with an extremely long, ribbon-like tail of black feathers. The **pink bill** is retained by the non-breeding male which resembles the drab, sparrow-like female. Male is usually accompanied by a harem of up to six females. Eggs are laid in the nest of the **Common Waxbill**. Favours open habitats, often near water.
Length: 12 cm (plus 22 cm tail in breeding male)
ss: Paradise Whydah (ochre below, broad tail)

## Redbilled Buffalo-weaver

Large weaver. Male is black with **pink bill** and white wing 'windows'. Female is pale ash-brown with a scaly appearance to the breast. Flocks nest communally in a large structure of thorny twigs, set in outer branches of large trees such as a Baobab. Seeds and small insects are eaten on the ground; often in company of starlings. Call is a jumbled chatter. Prone to nomadic movements.
Length: 24 cm  ss: Thickbilled Weaver (18 cm)

## Greyheaded Sparrow

Chestnut-backed sparrow with **plain grey head**, off-white underparts and narrow white wing bar. The bill is dark when breeding, paler in winter. Occurs in pairs or family groups in well-wooded areas. May form larger flocks in winter. Seeds and small insects are gathered on the ground. Call is a soft 'chirrp-chirrp'. Breeds in a tree hole.
Length: 15 cm  ss: Yellowthroated Sparrow (white eyebrow); House Sparrow (human settlements)

JOHN CARLYON

## Redbilled Quelea

Small finch. Male in breeding dress has a black mask surrounded by pink or ochre wash, and a **coral-red bill**. Females and non-breeding males are sparrow-like, but also have a red bill. Highly gregarious – flocks of several thousand are common-place. Breeds colonially; woven nests are hung from thorn trees. Raptors, storks and snakes prey on nestlings at noisy colonies. Nomadic.
Length: 13 cm

WILDERNESS SAFARIS/COLIN BELL

## Wattled Starling

Small, cream-buff starling with black wings and tail and distinctive **white rump**. When breeding some males have a bare yellow head adorned with black leathery wattles. Extremely gregarious, occurring in flocks of up to several hundred. Call is a variety of cackles and hisses. Feeds mostly on grasshoppers and prone to nomadic movements. Clustered stick nests are conspicuous.
Length: 21 cm

75

## Tawnyflanked Prinia

Tiny, **long-tailed** bird which frequents marshy ground and rank growth near water, but also enters dryland thickets. The **russet wings** and white eye-stripe are distinctive, as is its habit of raising its tail vertically. When disturbed it perches in an exposed position and utters its scolding 'sbee-sbee' call; often unafraid of people. Also has a 'tritt-tritt-tritt' call.

Length: 14 cm  ss: Neddicky (11 cm, short tail)

## Longbilled Crombec

Tiny, grey-brown bird with buffy under-parts and **short, almost non-existent tail**. The thin bill is down-curved. Occurs in pairs, often in the company of other species in mixed bird parties. Moves restlessly among foliage, often hanging upside-down to explore bark for insects. Call is a persistent 'chree-rit'.

Length: 12 cm  ss: Burntnecked Eremomela (10 cm, faint chestnut throat bar, sizeable tail); Grey Penduline Tit (8 cm)

## Rattling Cisticola

Dryland cisticola with rufous upperparts streaked in black, and pale underparts. Noisy and conspicuous, it perches on low bushes or in rank grass. The call is a distinctive 'tchi-tchi-tchi-trrrrrrrr'. Prefers open woodland. The similar **Wailing Cisticola** is restricted to rocky grass-land; the **Blackbacked Cisticola** is more boldly marked on the back and confined to wetlands.

Length: 13 cm  ss: Wailing Cisticola

## Redfaced Cisticola

Semi-aquatic cisticola with **plain rufous back** and creamy-white underparts. The face is rusty-red during the non-breeding season. Secretive but noisy, the piercing call – 'whee-chee-chee-cheer-cheer' – is a familiar sound in **reedbeds and rank growth near water**. Differs from all semi-aquatic warblers with its buff-tipped tail. The similar **Lazy Cisticola** is restricted to dry rocky areas.

Length: 13 cm  ss: Lazy Cisticola

## Yellowbreasted Apalis

Tiny, **long-tailed** bird which favours well-wooded habitats. The back is olive, the crown and face are grey and the underparts white with a broad, **lemon-yellow breast**. Males have a small black patch or bar on the chest. Moves restlessly among foliage in search of small insects. Usually occurs in pairs, and often joins mixed bird parties. The typical call is an urgent 'chizzick-chizzick-chizzick'.
Length: 13 cm  ss: Barthroated Apalis (pale eyes)

## Greenbacked Bleating Warbler

Tiny, green-backed bird with pale underparts and **olive-green wings and back**. Lively and restless, the tail is constantly flicked and raised to reveal the white vent. Occurs singly or in pairs in dense undergrowth, often near the ground; secretive and seldom seen. Extremely vociferous, the call is a bleating 'bleeep-bleeep' or 'chirrup-chirrup' – surprisingly strident for so small a bird.

Length: 12 cm  ss: Greybacked Bleating Warbler

LEX HES

## Cape White-eye

Tiny green bird with a distinctive **ring of small white feathers around the eyes**. Occurs in pairs during the summer breeding season but small flocks form in winter. Feeds on small insects, such as aphids, as well as berries. In the KNP, mostly confined to the area south of the Sabie River; but common in gardens of towns. Call is a soft musical warble. Often roosts in a huddle at night.
Length: 12 cm  ss: Yellow White-eye (far north)

## Yelloweyed Canary

Small canary with olive back and bright yellow underparts. Contrary to its name, the eye is black; a dark stripe runs from the bill to each eye and highlights the distinctive **yellow eyes-tripe**. The **bright yellow rump** is obvious in flight. Breeding male is brighter yellow below. Occurs in small flocks which feed quietly on the ground. Drinks regularly. Call is a soft swizzle or a chirpy song.
Length: 12 cm  ss: Bully Canary (15 cm, large bill)

LEX HES

RF EF

## Collared Sunbird

Tiny, metallic-green sunbird with **bright yellow underparts**. The male has a green throat terminating in a blue and purple band. The bill is shorter than that of other sunbirds. Occurs in pairs or family groups in tangled vegetation, often joining mixed bird parties. Frequently visits gardens. Feeds on small insects and nectar of flowers. Inconspicuous and quiet, the call is a soft 'tswee' or a chirpy song.
Length: 10 cm

LEX HES

B T EF RF

## Whitebellied Sunbird

Tiny sunbird with sexes not alike. The male is **metallic blue-green** on the back and head with a purple-blue throat and **snow-white belly**. The female is grey above, with unstreaked white underparts. The nest is a purse of leaves bound with spider webs. Feeds primarily on the nectar of tubular flowers. Frequently seen in gardens and KNP restcamps. Call is a strident, tinkling warble.
Length: 11 cm

T B

## Marico Sunbird

Small sunbird with the sexes not alike. The male is **metallic green** on the back, head and throat, with a claret breast and **black underparts**. The female is dull brown above and heavily streaked on the throat. Occurs in pairs in all habitats, and is frequently seen in KNP restcamps. Feeds mostly on nectar, but also takes small spiders and insects. Call is a fast swizzling warble.
Length: 14 cm  ss: Purplebanded Sunbird (12 cm)

RF T EF

## Scarletchested Sunbird

Medium-sized sunbird with the sexes not alike. The male is uniform dark brown, appearing black, with **bright scarlet chest** and iridescent turquoise forehead and throat. The female is dark brown above and mottled below. Often visits gardens. Feeds mostly on nectar, but also takes insects. Call is a repetitive 'cheep-chip-chop'. Male **Black Sunbird** has violet throat and rump, and emerald forehead; female lightly streaked below.
Length: 16 cm  ss: Black Sunbird (16 cm)

## Blue Waxbill

Tiny finch. The male has a brown back and **powder-blue face, underparts, rump and tail**. The female is paler on the back with a paler blue face and breast, and cream underparts. Occurs in pairs or small flocks in a variety of habitats, but most common in dry acacia scrub. Feeds on the ground, often in the company of other small seed-eaters. Call is a soft but high-pitched whistle.
Length: 13 cm  ss: Common Waxbill (red bill)

NATIONAL PARKS BOARD OF S.A.

G  B

## Redbilled Firefinch

Tiny finch. The male is pale crimson on the face and underparts with a sandy-brown back. A thin yellow ring encircles each dark eye. Female is sandy-brown above with fawn underparts. Both sexes have a pale red bill, **crimson rump** and tiny white spots on the breast and flanks. Feeds on the ground, often with wax-bills, in pairs or small flocks.
Length: 10 cm  ss: Jameson's Firefinch (grey bill); Bluebilled Firefinch (dark head and back, grey bill)

JOHN CARLYON

G  B

## Bronze Mannikin

Tiny, chocolate-brown finch with white underparts, black head and **pale lower bill**. The iridescent, green-bronze shoulders are not always obvious. Sexes are alike. Immature birds are buffy-fawn. Occurs in pairs or small flocks. Very restless. Feeds on grass seeds, often picking these up from the ground, and will also visit bird tables. Drinks regularly. Call is a soft, rasping warble.
Length: 9 cm  ss: Redbacked Mannikin (9 cm)

LEX HES

RW  EF

## Melba Finch

Tiny finch. The male is striking with a **scarlet bill, forehead, throat and tail**. The back is olive, head pale grey, and the underparts are finely barred in black and white. The female is duller, with no red on the face. Usually occurs in pairs, often in the company of other small seed-eaters. Feeds on the ground. Usual call is a single 'wik' note, but it sometimes warbles a lively song.
Length: 12 cm

G  B

# Reptiles

A wide variety of tortoises, terrapins, snakes and lizards occur in the Lowveld. Most reptiles are shy, however, and rather difficult to observe and study in the wild, particularly in the national parks where walking opportunities are limited. All reptiles are cold-blooded and require food less often than mammals or birds. Many become dormant and hibernate during the cool winter months. They are among the most misunderstood and feared of all animals, which is a great pity, as most are fascinating and harmless.

Reptiles are usually encountered by chance, but certain species are restricted to particular habitats and may be actively looked for. Many lizards – including the brilliantly coloured Common Flat Lizard and Rainbow Skink – favour exposed rocky areas, geckos favour walls or tree bark, and the Serrated Hinged Terrapin, Water Monitor and Nile Crocodile are confined to aquatic habitats.

Most snakes are nocturnal and seldom seen. Several potentially lethal venomous species occur – including the Black Mamba and Egyptian Cobra – but they will usually only bite in defence, and then as a last resort. If confronted by a snake, the best strategy is to remain calm and allow it every possible avenue of escape; any attempt to catch or kill it will only increase your chances of being bitten.

The names used in this section follow those in the *Field Guide to the Snakes and Other Reptiles of Southern Africa* by Bill Branch (Struik, 1988) – the most comprehensive and compact reference book for the region. *The Reptiles of the Kruger National Park* by Pienaar, Haake and Jacobsen (National Parks Board of South Africa, 1983) is a useful regional guide.

## Leopard Tortoise

Large tortoise with dull, dome-shaped shell which is neither hinged nor serrated on its rim. Adults weigh between 8 and 12 kg. Moves slowly about a home range of between 1 and 2 km², feeding on plant foliage and berries. Females lay clutches of ping-pong ball-sized eggs in shallow burrows. Young are vulnerable to predators such as Ground Hornbill, and adults to grass fires.
Length: up to 45 cm (max. 72 cm)

## Speke's Hinged Tortoise

Medium-sized tortoise with **flattened carapace** having a **distinctive hinge** which affords protection to its rump. The adult male is uniform sandy-brown while the female has darker edges to each carapace segment. Like all tortoises, the head is withdrawn into the shell when danger threatens. Most active after rain; feeds on berries, mushrooms, snails and millipedes. Hibernates during winter.
Length: 12 to 17 cm

## Serrated Hinged Terrapin

Large, blackish-brown terrapin with a
**domed carapace**. A hinge on the undersurface (plastron) serves to protect the
head. Occurs in perennial rivers, dams
and permanent waterholes where it basks
in the sun on branches or rocks with
neck outstretched. Diet includes freshwater mussels, frogs and carrion, and it
will also bite ticks off drinking buffalo.
Length: 30 to 40 cm  ss: Marsh Terrapin (30 cm;
flattened carapace, frequents seasonal pans only)

## Nile Crocodile

Massive aquatic predator which may live
to a great age. Juveniles feed on small
animals such as frogs; older crocodiles
take large fish and mammals up to the
size of impala. Egg clutches are laid in a
sand burrow, and young are guarded by
the female. Apparently more common in
the silt-laden waters of the Olifants and
Levuvhu rivers. May travel overland at
night during wet conditions.
Length: 3 to 4 m  (max. 6 m)

## Water Monitor

Massive **aquatic** lizard with an **elongated
snout**. Adults are dark olive-brown or
grey-brown on the back, and paler below.
Juveniles are patterned in yellow and
black. Feeds on anything it can over-
power, including crabs, frogs, and the
eggs of crocodiles and birds. Females
lay 20 to 60 soft-shelled eggs in a hole in
an active termite mound. The strong tail
is used in defence.
Length: 1 to 2 m

## Rock Monitor

Massive, **dry-land** lizard with a **rounded
snout**. Often **climbs trees**. Adults are
grey-brown on the back with pale blotches,
and pale yellow below with dark spots and
bands. Juveniles are more brightly
coloured. Feeds on anything it can over-
power, and also scavenges. Up to 30
soft-shelled eggs are laid – usually in a
self-excavated hole. The Martial Eagle is
its main predator.
Length: up to 1 m

EF  RO  B  T

81

### Giant Plated Lizard
Large, strongly armoured lizard with a long tapering tail. The dark, blackish-brown scales have small yellow spots which give a vaguely barred pattern. Juveniles are strikingly patterned with a blueish-black body spotted and striped in pale yellow. Occurs singly or in pairs on granite outcrops. Very shy and quick to retreat into cover. Feeds mostly on invertebrates and berries.
Length: 40 to 60 cm

### Roughscaled Plated Lizard
Medium-sized, strongly armoured lizard with **overlapping scales**. Body colour varies from pale brown to tawny, usually lighter below. Juveniles resemble adults. Occurs singly or in pairs, being most common in rocky areas where it finds refuge among crevices. May also live in small burrows in termite mounds. Feeds mostly on invertebrates and berries, but may catch larger prey.
Length: 30 to 40 cm

WD HAACKE

### Common Flat Lizard
Small, brightly coloured lizard with **compressed body** and triangular head. The generic name – *Platysaurus* – recalls the dinosaur age. The **male is dazzling with blue-green head and back, orange tail and blue throat** and under-side. **Females are blackish with three pale stripes on the back**. Occurs in pairs or colonies on exposed rocky out-crops. Feeds on ants and other insects.
Length: 18 to 28 cm

### Tree Agama
Medium-sized, tree-dwelling lizard with **large head**. The tip of the tail is readily shed to evade capture. Breeding male has a bright **cobalt-blue head**. The grey-brown skin of the female and non-breeding male provide cryptic camouflage against the bark of trees. The males bobs its head during display. Comes to ground only to move from one tree to another. Termites and ants are the main prey.
Length: 20 to 35 cm  ss: Ground Agama (20 cm)

82

## Rainbow Skink

Sleek, medium-sized lizard with long tapering tail. The male is buffy brown on the head and back with greenish flanks and **yellow-orange tail**; each scale has a tiny white spot and the whole **body glitters in the sunlight**. Females are darker, with striped flanks and a thin pale stripe down the back; the **tail is sky blue**. Immatures resemble the female but have an **electric blue tail**. Occurs in pairs among rocks.
Length: 18 to 24 cm

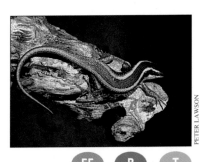

## Striped Skink

Small, dark, shiny lizard, with a long tapered tail. Active by day, it **keeps mostly to trees**, but is found in a wide variety of habitats. It often lives around buildings. Beetles and other insect prey are captured after a chase. Young are born live, and do not hatch from eggs. The closely related **Variegated Skink** is pale sandy-grey with darker speckles on the back, and rarely climbs trees.
Length: 20 cm  ss: Variegated Skink (14 cm)

PETER LAWSON

EF  B  T

## Common Dwarf Gecko

Tiny gecko, which is **active by day**. It lives on the trunks and branches of trees, but can be common on the outdoor walls of buildings. Termites, ants and other insects are the prey. Males are territorial. A pair of tiny, hard-shelled eggs are laid in cracks or crevices. The similarly sized **Speckled Gecko** is dark brown with tiny yellow spots on the back; it is largely **nocturnal**.
Length: 6 cm  ss: Speckled Gecko (7 cm)

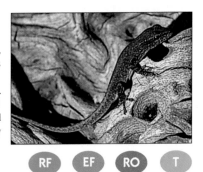

RF  EF  RO  T

## Tropical House Gecko

Chubby, **nocturnal** gecko which lives under the bark of trees, but often takes up residence in buildings where it hunts moths and other insects around lights. The scales on the **flat toes** have minute hairs which allow it to cling to smooth surfaces. The body is pale grey to pink-brown with darker bars. Males may fight vigorously and often lose their tail tips. A single tiny egg is 'glued' into a crevice.
Length: 14 cm  ss: Wahlberg's Velvet Gecko (16 cm)

RO  EF  RF

B  T  EF

## Flapnecked Chameleon

Distinctive reptile with big rounded head and **conical eyes**. The tail is often curled up. Adults are usually green, but are able to change colour to match foliage, bark or soil. Slow-moving, it is **active by day**. Most conspicuous when on the move after rain. A clutch of 25 to 50 eggs is buried in soil. Flies and other insects are caught with the long sticky tongue. Snakes are the main predators.
Length: 20 to 24 cm

PETER HANCOCK

RO  T  B  RW

## African Rock Python

Huge thick snake with geometrically patterned skin. Swims well and is fond of marshes. Adults may reach a great size, and are able to capture, squeeze and swallow prey up to the size of small antelope. May be common in sugarcane plantations. Although not poisonous, it may inflict a severe ripping bite with its fangs. Most active at dusk and after dark. Up to 50 large eggs are laid in a burrow.
Length: up to 5 m

C & T STUART

B  T  EF

## Brown House Snake

Large, thick-bodied snake which occurs in most habitats, and also in buildings where it preys on rodents. The squared-off snout and **two pale lines on either side of the pale eye** are diagnostic. Body colour is variable, ranging from light brown to rust, becoming darker with age. Prey is killed by constriction, then swallowed head first. Nocturnal. Up to 15 eggs are laid in summer.
Length: up to 1 m (max. 1.5 m)

B  T  EF

## Black Mamba ☠

Large sleek snake with a coffin-shaped head and permanent 'smile' created by its wide mouth. Body colour varies from dusky-olive to ash-grey, but is never black. Feeds mostly on birds and small mammals. Strongly territorial. Greatly feared, but will readily retreat if allowed to do so. If cornered it will strike repeatedly and even a small dose of venom is usually fatal to man.
Length: 2 to 3 m  (max. 4.3 m)

## Mozambique Spitting Cobra 🕱

Fairly large, thick-bodied snake. Forages on the ground, preying mostly upon rodents and toads. When threatened it rears up and spreads its hood; it may then **eject venom** into the eyes of an adversary. Colour varies from olive-brown to pale grey, with a pinkish belly and black throat. Most active after dark, often near water. Lives in termite mounds or under buildings. Also known as the 'Mfesi'.
Length: 1 to 1.2 m (max. 1.5 m)

PETER LAWSON

EF    T    B

## Snouted (Egyptian) Cobra 🕱

Large, thick-bodied snake with variable colouration. Most individuals are sandy-olive above and paler below; some may be dark brown and others banded on the back and tail. Nocturnal, but may be seen basking in the sun in the early morning. Unlike the previous species it **does not eject venom**, but will readily bite if cornered. Feeds on a variety of vertebrates including frogs and smaller snakes.
Length: 1.5 to 2 m (max. 2.4 m)

RO    T    B

## Olive Grass Snake 🕱

Fairly large, robust snake; sandy-brown above and pale yellow below. The **lip and underside is often finely spotted in black**. Occurs in open grassland or scrub but is partial to marshes. Preys mostly on rodents and frogs, but smaller snakes are occasionally eaten. This is a potentially dangerous species which bites readily and injects a painful venom. Primarily nocturnal.
Length: 1 to 1.3 m (max. 1.7 m)

PETER LAWSON

RW    EF    B    G

## Puff Adder 🕱

Stocky snake with chevron patterns in ochre, tan and black. The scales are keeled, giving a rough appearance and texture. Although most active at dusk and after dark, it may be seen during the day. Rodents, frogs and ground birds are the main prey. Litters consist of 20 to 40 young. It is sluggish and will bite readily, usually below the knee. The venom is potentially fatal to man.
Length: 70 to 90 cm (max. 1.2 m)

PETER LAWSON

RO    EF    G    B

## Boomslang (Tree Snake) 🐍

Fairly large, but thin snake characterised by **big eyes**. It is variable in colour. Males are bright or dull green with some black and pale blue markings. Females are pale olive-brown. Juveniles are greyish with a white chin, yellow throat and green eyes. Active by day, it feeds mostly on birds and chameleons. Shy, but extremely dangerous if handled – the venom may prove fatal to man.
Length: 1 to 2 m

**T** **RF** **EF** **B**

PETER LAWSON

## Spotted Bush Snake

Slender snake varying from dull olive to bright emerald in colour, with black spots and bars. The head is rather flat in shape. Active by day, it moves swiftly through and up trees in search of small geckos, chameleons and tree frogs. When agitated or threatened, it may inflate its neck to reveal bright blue skin, and strike out. Lacking fangs and venom glands, it is harmless to man.
Length: up to 1 m

**T** **RF** **EF** **B**

## Vine (Twig) Snake 🐍

Slender snake with a distinctive **pointed head** and **red tongue with black tip**. The skin is intricately patterned and serves as superb camouflage. Active by day, it waits in ambush for chameleons, geckos and small birds. Prey is swallowed as the snake dangles off a branch. Unless handled, bites are improbable, but the venom is highly toxic and potentially fatal to humans.
Length: up to 1 m

**T** **RF** **EF** **B**

## Herald (Redlipped) Snake

Small slender snake with glossy, blue-black head and **orange-red upper lip**. The body is uniform olive-brown above, sometimes with small white spots; the underbelly is off-white. **Nocturnal**. It feeds primarily upon frogs so is most frequent close to water. It has adapted well to human settlements and often lives in gardens and restcamps. Up to 12 eggs are laid in summer.
Length: 60 to 75 cm (max. 80 cm)

**RF** **RW** **EF**

# Frogs

The Lowveld has a rich diversity of frogs, with approximately forty species occurring in a variety of habitats. It may come as a surprise to learn that not all frogs depend upon permanent water – many species are adapted to dry habitats and emerge only after rain to breed in temporary pans. The 18 species featured here include those which are most often encountered.

Frogs have two stages in life: the tadpole (larval), which is usually totally aquatic, and the four-limbed adult, which may be active in and out of water. Several species exhibit unusual breeding behaviour.

Like birds, frogs have distinctive calls and this facilitates their identification and study. Most species are only active after dark, however, and are best found by going out at night with a strong torch after, or during, rain. A wide variety of frog species may be found in the restcamps of the Kruger National Park, including some – such as the Foamnest Frog – which frequently enter buildings. Remember that snakes have as much interest in frogs as any naturalist so take care when out 'frogging' at night. Some species of frog, especially the Red Toad, enter rooms and tents to hunt insects and may seek refuge inside shoes (as will numerous other creatures); if camping, it is wise to shake your shoes out before putting them on in the morning!

The names used in this section follow those in *South African Frogs – A Complete Guide* (Southern and Wits Univ. Press, 1995) by Neville Passmore and Vincent Carruthers; this book also includes information on frog ecology. A compact disc entitled *Voices of South African Frogs* supplements this work.

## Tropical Platanna

Extraordinary frog with a compressed body and **eyes on the top of its head**. Usually seen suspended just below the water surface. It is almost totally aquatic, but may move about during rain. The fore limbs are short and slender, but the hind legs are large and powerful with webbing between the **clawed toes**. Preys upon small fish, insects and tadpoles, and will also scavenge. Said to call underwater.
Length: 5 to 8 cm  ss: Common Platanna

## African Bullfrog

Large, olive-green or brown frog with pale armpits and yellow throat. Remains underground in winter, but numbers emerge after heavy summer rains to occupy temporary pans. They produce large numbers of eggs which develop rapidly before the water dries up. Preys upon insects and other frogs and some-times cannibalises its own young. The call is a low 'whoop'.
Length: 8 to 14 cm

87

VINCENT CARRUTHERS

## Olive Toad

Sandy-brown or grey toad with reddish patches but an **unmarked snout**. Like the Guttural Toad it may have red flecks on the thighs. Rain stimulated breeding occurs in temporary pans and marshes or garden ponds. The **call is a loud bray**, repeated at one second intervals by groups of males from exposed positions at the water's edge. May gather in groups to feed on termites.

Length: 5 to 7 cm  ss: Flatbacked Toad (6 cm)

B  RW  EF

VINCENT CARRUTHERS

## Guttural Toad

Brown or grey toad with **dark patches including a pair on the snout**, and red, blood-like flecks on the thighs. Breeds in permanent water but often forages some distance away and can be seen around outdoor lights after dark. The **call is a reverberating snore** often uttered in chorus by numerous males at the water's edge. Begins calling in early spring. May gather in groups to feed on termites.

Length: 5 to 7 cm

B  RW  EF

VINCENT CARRUTHERS

## Red Toad

Grey or brick-red toad distinguished by a **raised dark line down its side** running from eye to groin. Two dark spots may be present on the back. Breeds in temporary pans and dams where males indulge in bouts of chorusing; the repetitive **call can be likened to the revs of a large motorbike** and is usually made whilst afloat. Nocturnal, but may be active on cloudy days. Often found in gardens and homes.

Length: 5 to 7 cm

EF  B  RW

## Natal Sand Frog

Small burrowing frog with a toad-like shape and posture. A **small flat disc is present on each hind foot**. One of the noisiest of all frogs, the male calls with a **loud, monotonous piping note** from an exposed position on sandbanks or around pools. Mostly nocturnal but may call on overcast days in spring. Similar **Tremelo Sand Frog** and **Russetbacked Sand Frog** both have a blunt snout.

Length: 3 to 4 cm  ss: Tremelo Sand Frog

EF

## Ornate Frog

Medium-sized frog which spends most of its time in an underground burrow and is usually only encountered after rain. The back is beautifully patterned with **chocolate and cream blotches** and a **variable amount of lime green**. In common with the sand frogs, the front fingers are free of webbing. Breeds in seasonal pans and vleis. **Call is a nasal quack**, repeated every two seconds.
Length: 5 cm

## Banded Rubber Frog

Medium-sized, rather flat frog. The black body is smooth, almost shiny, with broad bands of red, pink or yellow on the back, and small spots on the legs. These bright warning colours advise would-be predators of its unpalatability; the skin is said to exude toxins. Most frequent in seasonal, rain-filled pans. Males sit at the water's edge and **call with a loud, telephone-like trill**.
Length: 5 to 6 cm

## Bushveld Rain Frog

Tiny rotund frog with a down-turned mouth which gives it a permanently grumpy appearance. The back is mottled in various shades of brown, tan and buff, and the underparts are white. It spends most of its life underground in a torpid state, emerging (often in large numbers) after rain. Eggs are laid underground, and the tadpoles live in moist chambers until they change into froglets.
Length: 3 to 4 cm

## Common River Frog (Rana)

Slender, green or brown frog with dark spots and blotches. The **snout is pointed** and the **hind legs are very long and powerful**. Occurs in perennial streams and permanent dams and ponds. Often sits on emergent stones or at the water's edge, but is quick to dive in with a splash if disturbed. **Call is a distinctive rattle and croak**, uttered mostly on cool winter nights.
Length: 5 to 7 cm

89

## Broadbanded Grass Frog

Small streamlined frog with powerful hind legs and pointed snout. The back is **variable in colour** but always has a **pale central band**. Up to six raised ridges run down the back. May be abundant in wet grassland but is easily overlooked. **Call is a nasal quack** repeated continuously. The similar **Plain Grass Frog** is uniform brownish-pink on the back; the call is a high-pitched trill.

Length: 5 cm  ss: Plain and Sharpnosed grass frogs

## Common Caco

Tiny squat frog which is most active after rain. The body colour is extremely variable, ranging from emerald-green to dull brown. Stripes, blotches and spots may be present. If caught, the **white underbelly with dark spots** is diagnostic. Numbers gather at temporary pans and pools to breed; the **piercing click call** is uttered monotonously at night and on cloudy days. Secretive.

Length: 2 cm  ss: Snoring Puddle Frog

## Bubbling Kassina

Small, boldly patterned frog. The back is variable in colour, being fawn, yellow or olive, but the bold dark stripes are distinctive. The sides are mottled and the underbelly is off-white. Most common around seasonal pans but is seldom seen due to its retiring habits. The **call is a loud liquid 'quoip'**, made during the day or night from the base of a grass tuft, often some distance from water.

Length: 5 to 6 cm  ss: Redlegged Kassina

## Brownbacked Tree Frog

Small frog with broad head and large bulging eyes. The limbs are slender, with toes and fingers terminating in adhesive discs. Adults are tawny-brown on the back with dark streaks; immatures pale green. The **call is a loud nasal 'ka-wak'**, repeated at intervals from an elevated perch in a tree or bush. Eggs are laid among damp vegetation or leaves near streams or pans. Nocturnal.

Length: 4 to 5 cm

## Foamnest Frog

Medium-sized frog with slender, webbed toes tipped with adhesive pads. It lives in the branches of trees but **frequently enters buildings**. The body colour is variable in shades of grey or tan, but when sitting in sunlight the skin turns a chalky white. The eggs are laid in a foamy nest – whipped up by the mating couple and a gaggle of unpaired males – hung from a branch over a pool or pan.
Length: 5 to 6 cm

## Painted Reed Frog

Tiny, brightly coloured frog. Adults are **variable in colour**, with bodies **boldly striped in black, white, yellow and red**; some are olive-fawn. Flattened discs on the toe tips enable it to climb on slippery surfaces. Often abundant in reedbeds and rank growth on the edge of pans. The **monotonous, short whistle call** is made by day or night; many males calling simultaneously to create a noisy din.
Length: 2 to 3 cm

## Waterlily Frog

Tiny, translucent green frog with long, slender limbs. Some individuals have tiny black spots scattered on the back. The flattened discs on the toe tips enable it to climb on slippery surfaces. Occurs in pans and marshes where waterlilies or other floating plants grow. Males call from exposed positions and may be active by day but are well camouflaged; the **call is a soft squeaky chip**.
Length: 2 to 3 cm

## Golden Leaffolding Frog

Tiny, golden- or creamy-yellow frog with darker flanks. Closely resembles the reedfrogs in shape and habits, the limbs being slender and the toes terminating in adhesive discs. Occurs in pans and marshes alongside dams, where it repeats its **soft rattle call** from dusk into the night. The jelly-coated eggs are laid on an elongated leaf which is folded over and sealed to form an underwater tube.
Length: 2 cm

# Freshwater Fishes

Although rarely seen by visitors to the Kruger National Park and other wildlife reserves, nearly 50 fish species occur in the rivers, streams, pans and artificial dams of the Lowveld. Some of these fishes may be seen at the aquaculture station in Lydenburg (details on p. 123). Only a few of the more common fishes are featured here. Apart from being fascinating creatures in their own right, it should be remembered that fishes play a critical role in the ecology of aquatic habitats and are a vital link in the food chain for animals such as Nile Crocodile and African Fish Eagle.

Regrettably, there are numerous threats to the fishes of the Lowveld, even those within the borders of wildlife reserves. The greatest of these is the decreased flow of the region's rivers, which has reduced available habitat. This is due primarily to intensive agricultural practices in the catchment areas; citrus, sugarcane and timber plantations all draw large volumes of water and reduce stream flow. Chemical poisoning is an ever-present threat with insecticides and industrial effluent entering drainage systems; although fishes may not themselves be killed by such pollution, the invertebrates upon which they feed often are. Of further concern is the spread of alien aquatic plants such as Water Hyacinth *Eichhornia crassipes* and Kariba Weed *Salvinia molesta,* which diminish light and oxygen levels in water.

Names used in this section follow those in *A Complete Guide to the Freshwater Fishes of Southern Africa* by Paul Skelton (Southern, 1993) – the most comprehensive guide to the 245 indigenous and introduced species in southern Africa. *The Freshwater Fishes of the Kruger National Park* by U. de V Pienaar (National Parks Board of South Africa, 1968) is a useful regional guide.

PAUL SKELTON

## Longfin Eel

Large elongated fish with dorsal and anal fins joining to form the tail. The head and back is yellow-ochre, with paler underside. Occurs in deep pools where it preys upon crabs, fishes and frogs. The life cycle is remarkable with adults returning to the ocean to spawn, young 'glass eels' living in estuaries, and immature 'elvers' migrating inland up river courses; the cycle taking many years.
Length: 1.4 m  ss: Madagascar Mottled Eel

## Sharptooth Catfish (Barbel)

R A JUBB

Large predatory fish with compressed body, bony head and filament-like tendrils (barbels). Slate-grey above, white below. Fish of this *Clarias* genus are unique in being able to breath air. Reaches a greater size, and is more common, in murky waters. Often abundant in seasonal pans and pools, where they may become trapped and provide a feast for scavenging birds and mammals. Migrate to spawn in shallow waters during summer.
Length: up to 1.4 m  ss: Silver Catfish (30 cm)

## Bowstripe Barb

Small, **translucent**, olive-brown fish with a distinctive **bow-shaped black line** on each flank. One of 10 finger-sized fishes belonging to the *Barbus* genus in the area; also known as minnows. Most live in shoals which move as one, close to the surface of the water. Favours vegetated pools of streams and rivers, and the fringes of dams where it feeds on tiny aquatic invertebrates.

Length: 7 cm  ss: Beira Barb; Threespot Barb

PAUL SKELTON

## Rednosed Labeo (Mudfish)

Medium-sized fish with large, **sail-like dorsal fin**, and deeply cleft tail fin. The body colour is variable in shades of olive-bronze, pink and silvery-grey. The eyes and upper lips are rosy red. Occurs in waters with a sandy bottom, including isolated pools in seasonal streams. Feeds mostly on detritus and algae. A lively fish, it may leap some distance when netted; attractive angling species.

Length: 40 cm ss: Redeye Labeo; Leaden Labeo

## Tigerfish

Large silvery fish with **black stripes on the flanks**. The pointed fins are yellow or red. Sharply pointed teeth protrude from the strong jaws. Preys mostly upon small shoaling fish. Occurs only in larger rivers but breeds on the Mozambique flats; numbers in the KNP are thought to be declining due to dams and weirs which inhibit migration upstream. Bold and aggressive, it is a prized angling fish.

Length: 70 cm (female); 50 cm (male)

PAUL SKELTON

## Mozambique Tilapia

Medium-sized, omnivorous fish with a distinctive **long dorsal fin fringed with spines**. Adults are silvery-olive with dorsal and tail fins tipped in red; breeding male changes colour to dark grey-black with a white throat. Tolerant of various water conditions (including marine) but avoids fast-flowing streams. Male builds a bowl-shaped 'nest' on sandy bottoms, and the female broods eggs and young in her mouth. Prized by anglers.

Length: 40 cm  ss: Redbreast Tilapia; Banded Tilapia

R A JUBB

93

# Invertebrates

The animal kingdom is divided into two broad groupings. The 'higher' classes, from fishes to mammals, are typified by an internal skeleton and are known as *vertebrates*. The 'lower' classes lack an internal skeleton, are generally much smaller in size, and are known as *invertebrates*. There is an enormous number of different invertebrates and new species are constantly being identified.

The presence of so many impressive mammals and birds in the Lowveld diverts the attention of many people from the extraordinary diversity of invertebrates, of which the insects are perhaps the most abundant and note-worthy. The important ecological function of insects should not be underestimated: a great many bird species, as well as numerous mammals, are dependent upon them for their livelihood, and they perform the critical job of pollination for most flowering plants. Without insects, all life would grind to a halt. On a more mundane level, many insects cannot help but be noticed even by the most disinterested person, if only for their painful bite or incessant noise.

Many invertebrates are fascinating subjects to observe and they usually allow a more intimate examination of their lives than do larger animals. Exploring vegetation in restcamps and gardens, or sitting quietly at a pond or waterhole, will reveal many interesting insects, spiders and other invertebrates. A small magnifying glass (8x or 10x is ideal) and a glass jar for temporarily housing specimens will aid study. Insects and other invertebrates make excellent photographic subjects, but a macro lens or more specialised equipment is required.

Only a few of the more interesting or noticeable invertebrates are featured here, and all – except the colourful butterflies and moths – are identified to family level only. Habitat symbols have been excluded in order to feature more families.

A list of more detailed publications relating to invertebrates is provided on p. 122. The best general text on insects is *African Insect Life* by Skaife and revised by John Ledger (Struik, 1988). The pocket-sized *Field Guide to Insects of the Kruger National Park* by Leo Braack (Struik, 1991) provides a good introduction to the more conspicuous families. *Butterflies of Southern Africa – A Field Guide* by Mark Williams (Southern, 1994) is an easy-to-use guide to the most frequently encountered butterfly species.

### Giant land snail

Large dryland snail which is usually only encountered after rain. Mostly nocturnal. The shells of dead snails, which turn white with age, are often found. Preyed upon by reptiles, birds and even hyenas.

### Millipedes

Long cylindrical arthropods with hair-like legs. Movement is slow, but they are avoided by most predators as they eject a pungent, toxic fluid. Curl into a spiral if threatened. Usually black.

## Orbweb spiders

Large, usually yellow and black spiders which construct hanging webs to trap prey. The webs of some are gold in colour, and strong enough to hold small birds. Male is tiny compared to female.

## Jumping spiders

Small, ground-living spiders with large obvious eyes. No web is made. Small insects such as flies and ants are pounced upon after a stalk. Some species mimic ants in colour and shape.

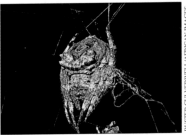

## Flower crab spiders

Small, triangular-bodied spiders which ambush insect prey in flowers. Colour varies according to flowers in which they choose to sit, with pink, white and yellow forms being most common.

## Bark spiders

Medium-sized, cryptically coloured spiders which build large hanging webs strung between trees. The webs are built at night, when the spiders may be seen by torchlight, but are dismantled by day.

## Scorpions

Eight-legged arachnids with large pincers and sting-tipped tail curved over the body. Prey on insects. Most species are nocturnal. Those with small pincers and fat tails have the most toxic venom.

## Ticks

Small, eight-legged relatives of spiders. They become engorged after feeding on the blood of larger animals. May transmit diseases such as tick-bite fever. Should be looked for on skin after walking in grass.

**Dragonflies**

Small to large insects always associated with open water. Many species are brightly coloured in red or green. Wings are held at right angles to the body when at rest. Predator. Larvae develop in water.

**Cicadas**

Cryptically coloured bugs which are rarely seen due to their remarkable camouflage. Males make an incessant and shrill noise on hot summer days and evenings. All are sap suckers.

LEX HES

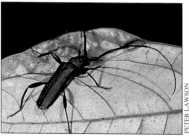

PETER LAWSON

**Dung beetles**

Distinctive beetles with extremely powerful hind limbs and a flat shield on the snout. Adults are attracted to animal dung, rolling balls away backwards. Eggs are laid in dung balls.

**Longhorn beetles (borers)**

Small to large beetles with distinctive antennae often longer than their body. Adults deposit eggs into decaying wood and the larval grubs tunnel their way out, eating wood in the process.

LEX HES

LEX HES

**Termites**

Tiny herbivorous insects with a complex social order. Colonies consist of a 'queen', sterile workers, sterile soldiers and winged reproductives (alates) which emerge after rain. Most build mounds.

**Ants**

Tiny gregarious insects which are usually black or red in colour. Colonies consist of a 'queen', workers and soldiers. Most are carnivorous, but some feed on sap or 'honeydew' secreted by aphids.

## Praying mantids

Predatory insects with distinctive enlarged forelimbs used to capture flies and beetles. Well camouflaged in shades of green or pink. Females are larger than males. Often feeds around light at night.

## Grasshoppers

Herbivorous insects with powerful hind legs held in an inverted V-shape above the cigar-shaped body. Several species are brightly coloured. Locusts are migratory, swarm-forming grasshoppers.

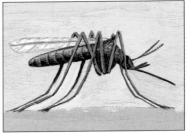

## Blow flies

Small flies, usually metallic-blue or green with orange eyes. Feed on carrion, around which they may gather in large swarms. Adults may also lay eggs in the flesh of living animals.

## Mosquitoes

Tiny, fly-like insects. Only females suck blood and make the irritating whining noise. Males are silent and feed on plant sap. Eggs are laid in still water. Some species transmit malaria.

## Honey bees

Small gregarious insects which feed on nectar and are attracted in large numbers to flowering plants. Complex social order, with a colony building a hive in a tree hole. Sting is potentially dangerous.

## Paper wasps

Social wasps which build papery nests under overhangs such as ceilings. They deliver a painful sting. Larger *Belonogaster* have thin waists, smaller *Polistes* have a striped abdomen.

## Lunar Moth

Spectacular, pale green moth with extended 'tails' on the lower wings. In common with all moths the antennae are feathered. This is a nocturnal, nectar-feeding species, as are most other moths.

## Mopane Emperor Moth (larva)

Colourful caterpillar known as a 'Mopane Worm', which is the larva of a drab, pale brown moth. Feeds exclusively on the foliage of Mopane trees. Relished by many bird species and also by man.

## African Monarch

Rust-red butterfly with wings marked in black and white. In common with all butterflies, it is active by day and has thin clubbed antennae. Body fluid is toxic, so it is avoided by predators.

## Common Dotted Border

Medium-sized butterfly with characteristic bouncy flight usually a metre or so above the ground. Male is white above, female pale yellow; the underwing of both is yellow with an orange smear.

## African Migrant

Males are white above with pale green underwings; females are lemon-yellow above with tan wing tips, and mottled yellow below. May form large migratory flocks. Often drinks from puddles.

## Brownveined White

Small, predominantly white butterfly with brown patterns on the wings; females have a yellow wash. Large numbers migrate in flocks at the middle or end of summer.

## Whitebarred Charaxes

Large, fast-flying butterfly which usually perches high in trees but comes to ground to drink from puddles or suck fluid from carnivore dung. Upperside of wings are less boldly marked than the underside.

## Pearl Charaxes

Large, fast-flying butterfly with distinctive pale centre and coppery-red wings. Closed wings resemble a dried leaf. Territorial male perches high in a tree. Sips nectar from fruit and often drinks from puddles.

STEPHEN WOODHALL

## Citrus Swallowtail

Large, pale yellow butterfly with black patterning. Flies purposefully at medium height. The wings are kept moving when feeding on nectar. Territorial male resides in bush clumps and gardens.

## Greenbanded Swallowtail

Large, almost black butterfly with broad, blue-green bands down each wing. Flight is strong and direct, usually at about a metre off the ground. Favours shady situations.

## Common Orange Tip

Small, mostly white butterfly with orange-yellow tips to the forewings and a brown smudge between the wings. The female differs in having less white above. Active only in sunny weather.

LEX HES

## Yellow Pansy

Small, yellow and black butterfly with distinctive **blue wing spots**. It flies with a characteristic double wing beat followed by a glide on outstretched wings. Feeds on sap and moisture from dung.

# Trees and Woody Shrubs

A tremendous diversity of trees and shrubs occur in the Lowveld with close to 400 species found in the KNP alone. In this section 60 of the more familiar or impressive trees and shrubs are featured, with emphasis on those likely to be seen in the KNP. Much of the escarpment foothills have been encroached upon by invasive alien plants, the most conspicuous of which are included along with a few of the more striking ornamental (exotic but not invasive) trees.

The identification of trees and shrubs may pose problems for beginners, but one way of getting to know them is to **actively look for the more common species featured here**. Explore the area around restcamps and gardens where leaves, flowers and fruits are usually within reach, and where some specimens may be labelled. The Lowveld Botanical Garden has almost all of the indigenous species featured here in cultivation.

The recommended reference book is *Trees of Southern Africa* by Keith Coates Palgrave (Struik, 1977), but the *Field Guide to the Trees of the Kruger National Park* by Piet van Wyk (Struik, 1984) is a useful, and more compact, regional publication. Other useful books on trees and shrubs are listed on p. 122.

When beginning to identify trees, it is important to learn their scientific names, as any future study will involve comparison between related species; common names may be misleading as they often put species into families to which they do not belong. In most instances, the photographs illustrate only the leaves, and sometimes flowers and fruit, so the short, descriptive texts must be referred to for tree shape, bark and other details.

### *Phoenix reclinata*
#### Wild Date Palm/Wildedadelboom
Bushy palm with **dark green, feather-shaped leaves** up to 4 m long. Forms clumps along rivers and streams, and also grows on termite mounds. Clusters of creamy-white flowers are held in orange sheaths. Edible fruits appear in late summer; yellow ripening to brown. Birds, monkeys, African Civet and people eat fruit; elephants feed on the leaves.
ARECACEAE  Height: up to 6 m

### *Hyphaene coriacea*
#### Lala Palm/Lalapalm
Tall palm with **grey-green, fan-shaped leaves** up to 1.2 m wide. The petioles are armed with black spines. Fully grown, unbranched specimens are uncommon; usually forms impenetrable clumps in low-lying areas but not always along rivers. Most common north of the Letaba River. Small flowers appear in early summer. Clusters of large, bell-shaped fruits hang on the tree throughout the year.
ARECACEAE  Height: up to 15 m

## *Ficus sycomorus*
### Sycamore Fig/Gewone Trosvy

Massive spreading tree with smooth, pale
yellow trunk and branches. Invariably
grows near water or in low-lying areas.
Leaves coarse in texture. Contains milky
latex. Evergreen. Large figs are green,
ripening to orange; borne on branchlets
off main stems throughout the year.
Birds, bats, monkeys and insects are
among the animals which eat the figs.

MORACEAE Height: up to 20 m

## *Ficus thonningii*
### Strangler Fig/Gewone Wildevy

Large spreading tree with smooth, pale
grey bark. Often has aerial roots hanging
from branches and is **usually a strangler of other trees**. Leaves simple, dull
or glossy with **long petiole**; in droopy
spirals around stems. Contains milky
latex. Evergreen. Small stalkless figs are
massed along stems; relished by birds
and bats.

MORACEAE Height: up to 15 m

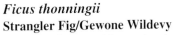

## *Ficus glumosa*
### Mountain Fig/Bergvy

Small to large tree with gnarled shape
and outstretched branches. Flaky bark
varies from almost white to grey or ochre.
**Young leaves and petioles are hairy**
but mature leaves shiny dark green above.
Small figs borne in leaf axils, clustered
at the end of stems. Common in rocky
hills south of the Sabie River and around
Nelspruit; also at Punda Maria.

MORACEAE Height: up to 12 m

## *Ficus abutilifolia*
### Largeleaved Rock Fig/Klipvy

Small tree which grows among rocks –
which it is able to split with its roots –
and on sheer cliffs. The stem and exposed
roots are pale yellow or grey-white; when
seen from a distance they appear to have
been poured over the rocks. **Leaves are
large, heart-shaped and glossy, with
prominent yellow veins**. Pale green figs
ripen to red; borne in leaf axils.

MORACEAE Height: up to 6 m

101

## *Acacia nigrescens*
### Knob Thorn/Knoppiesdoring
Tall upright tree with rounded crown. May be dominant in flat or undulating country. Bark is fissured and often **bears large, thorn-tipped knobs**. Leaves bipinnately compound with **leaflets larger than in any other acacia**. Thorns hook-shaped. Spikes of cream flowers cover the tree in early September. Pods are thin and papery. Deciduous.
MIMOSACEAE Height: up to 16 m

## *Acacia tortilis*
### Umbrella Thorn/Haak-en-steek
Large flat-topped tree with bare, low-branching trunk – the archetypal tree of African savannas. Largest specimens grow near rivers. **Bark is grey and vertically grooved**. Leaves bipinnately compound with tiny leaflets. **Both straight and hook-shaped thorns** are present. Flowers are cream balls in early summer. **Pods small, coiled in clusters**. Deciduous.
MIMOSACEAE Height: up to 12 m

## *Acacia sieberiana*
### Paperbark Thorn/Papierbasdoring
Large, flat-topped tree with bare, low-branching trunk. Abundant in foothills near Nelspruit; rare in the KNP. **Bark is corky, pale yellow**; peels off in papery sections. Leaves bipinnately compound with tiny leaflets. **Thorns straight, white**. Cream, ball-shaped flowers cover the tree in November. **Pods large, broad, pale sandy-brown**. Deciduous.
MIMOSACEAE Height: up to 12 m

## *Acacia nilotica*
### Scented Thorn/Lekkerruikpeul
Small bushy tree which may form an umbrella-shape. Most common in poorly drained soils where it often grows in dense thickets. Bark is dark grey and deeply grooved. Leaves bipinnately compound. Thorns straight, paired, often backward-pointing. **Distinctive 'beaded' pods** are sweet-scented, as are the yellow ball flowers which appear in summer.
MIMOSACEAE Height: up to 7 m

## *Acacia xanthophloea*
### Fever Tree/Koorsboom

Tall upright tree with sparse crown. The **sulphur-yellow bark**, powdery to the touch, is diagnostic. Grows along streams and rivers, and is widely cultivated in rest-camps and towns. Prefers the same habitat as the malaria-carrying mosquito – hence the name. Leaves bipinnately compound; thorns straight, paired white; yellow ball flowers in summer; pods sickle-shaped.
MIMOSACEAE  Height: up to 15 m

## *Acacia ataxacantha*
### Flame Thorn/Vlamdoring

Scrambling shrub which may climb to the tops of the tallest trees. Most conspicuous when covered with **crimson pods** at the end of summer. Occurs mostly along watercourses and in thickets where it may form an impenetrable barrier. Leaves bipin-nately compound, feathery; thorns hooked, not paired; flowers are cream spikes; pods are long and narrow.
MIMOSACEAE  Height: up to 5 m or more

## *Faidherbia albida* (= *Acacia albida*)
### Ana Tree/Anaboom

Tall upright tree which may grow to a great size; older trees have drooping branches. The only tree which is **usually leafless in summer**, it grows along river banks, mostly in the north. Young **stems are white with zig-zag growth pattern**; thorns straight in pairs; leaves bipinnately compound; cream spike flowers; thick, coiled pods eaten by many animals.
MIMOSACEAE  Height: up to 25 m

## *Dichrostachys cinerea*
### Sicklebush/Sekelbos

Small tree or shrub with **acacia-like** appearance. Usually multi-stemmed, often forms thickets. Widespread on sandy soils. Bark is grey-brown, deeply grooved. Leaves bipinnately compound with tiny leaflets. Thorns straight, dark brown. **Flowers are attractive pink and yellow catkins** during summer. Pods are twisted in bunches. Deciduous.
MIMOSACEAE  Height: up to 5 m

### *Colophospermum mopane*
### Mopane/Mopanie
Large, often V-shaped tree with rounded crown. Abundant and dominant on poorly drained clay soils, as tall single-species woodland or low scrub. Bark is grey and deeply furrowed. **Leaves are divided into a butterfly shape**; bright green when young, ageing to coppery-red. Flowers inconspicuous. Fruit is a thin, kidney-shaped pod. Deciduous.
CAESALPINIACEAE Height: up to 18 m

### *Schotia brachypetala*
### Weeping Boerbean/Huilboerboon
Large tree with a spreading crown. Usually grows on termite mounds or along watercourses; most common south of the Sabie River. Most conspicuous in September when **branches are massed with nectar-rich, blood-red flowers**. Compound leaves shiny green with 4 to 6 pairs of leaflets; woody pods. Loses leaves only for a brief period in spring.
CAESALPINIACEAE Height: up to 12 m

### *Afzelia quanzensis*
### Pod Mahogany/Peulmahonie
Large, deciduous tree with wide spreading crown. Stems and trunk are pale grey, bark flaking off in older trees. Common around Punda Maria and on the Lebombo Hills, and many planted in KNP restcamps. Compound leaves glossy green with 4 to 7 pairs of leaflets, margins wavy; **large woody pods** house **black and red seeds**; flowers have single pink petal.
CAESALPINIACEAE Height: up to 20 m

### *Bolusanthus speciosus*
### Tree Wisteria/Vanwykshout
Medium-sized, upright tree with drooping foliage. Often branches low down or may be multi-stemmed. Most striking in September when **mauve, pea-shaped flowers cover the tree** before or with new leaf growth. Bark is dark and deeply fissured. Compound leaves have 3 to 7 pairs of leaflets plus a terminal leaflet. Papery pods borne in clusters.
FABACEAE Height: 7 to 10 m

## *Lonchocarpus capassa*
### Rain Tree/Appelblaar

Tall, **irregularly shaped** tree with twisted
trunk and sparse foliage. Reaches greatest
size on alluvial soils; indicates high
water-table. Pale bark flakes off in blocks.
Leaves compound, with one or two pairs
of leaflets and terminal leaflet; frequently
eaten by insects. Flowers small, lilac,
pea-shaped in early summer. Pods thin,
papery, in clusters. Deciduous.
FABACEAE   Height: up to 18 m

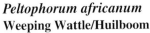

## *Peltophorum africanum*
### Weeping Wattle/Huilboom

Medium-sized, bushy tree with acacia-
like appearance but **no thorns**. Branches
low down or may be multi-stemmed.
Bark becomes rough grey-brown with age.
Leaves bipinnately compound, feathery,
fern-like. Yellow flowers showy with
crinkled petals in erect sprays; appear
November to December. Oval pods flat,
pale brown, in bunches. Deciduous.
CAESALPINIACEAE   Height: up to 10 m

## *Cassia abbreviata*
### Longtail Cassia/Sambokpeul

Small tree with sparse, spreading crown.
Remarkable for its **extremely long, tail-
like pods** which split and twist to reveal
seeds embedded in green pulp. Clusters
of showy yellow flowers appear in
August to September. Leaves compound,
with up to 11 pairs of leaflets; deciduous.
Bark of mature trees is dark brown to
black, divided into ridged blocks.
CAESALPINIACEAE   Height: up to 6 m

## *Pterocarpus angolensis*
### Kiaat/Bloedhout

Tall tree with sparse, spreading crown
of drooping leaves. Distinctive in winter
when leafless and decorated with **round,
papery-fringed pods with spiky centres**.
Prefers deep sandy soil; abundant near
Nelspruit and Pretoriuskop. Bark dark,
furrowed. Exudes **blood-red sap**. Leaves
compound with terminal leaflet. Small
yellow flowers in bunches in spring.
FABACEAE   Height: up to 16 m

## *Erythrina lysistemon*
### Coral Tree/Koraalboom
Medium-sized tree with rounded crown
which usually branches low down.
**Leafless and covered with spectacular
scarlet flowers** from June to August.
Occurs among rocks but planted in many
towns and KNP restcamps. Leaves trifoliate
with triangular leaflets; often attacked by
gall-forming insects. **Beaded pods contain
scarlet 'lucky beans'**. Thorns on stems.
FABACEAE Height: up to 12 m

## *Delonix regia* *
### Flamboyant
Large tree with short stem and spectacular
umbrella shape. Gnarled roots often
exposed. A **non-invasive** ornamental
**native to Madagascar**; planted in towns
and in Pretoriuskop restcamp. **Masses of
scarlet flowers** appear in November.
Leaves bipinnately compound with 8 to
15 pairs of leaflets. **Woody pods very
long and broad**. Deciduous.
CAESALPINIACEAE Height: up to 15 m

## *Bauhinia galpinii*
### Pride-of-De-Kaap/Vlaktevlam
Scrambling shrub favouring rocky hillsides or watercourses. Beautiful **brick-
red flowers** appear in profusion in mid-
summer. **Leaves two-lobed** and notched;
becoming yellow in autumn. Long
woody pods have pointed tips; split and
twist on the tree to release hard seeds.
Popular garden plant; grown in many
towns and KNP restcamps. Deciduous.
CAESALPINIACEAE Height: up to 5 m

## *Spathodea campanulata* *
### African Flame Tree
Large upright tree with **fluted trunk
buttressed at the base** in old specimens.
**Non-invasive** ornamental **native to
Tropical Africa**; planted in many towns.
Magnificent **orange-red, tulip-shaped
flowers** appear in summer. Cigar-shaped
fruits house papery seeds. Compound
leaves hairy with up to six pairs of
leaflets, plus a terminal leaflet.
BIGNONIACEAE Height: up to 20 m

## *Kigelia africana*
### Sausage Tree/Worsboom

Large deciduous tree with a short squat trunk. Most common along river banks, widely planted in KNP restcamps. The compound leaves have up to four pairs of leaflets and terminal leaflet; crusty in texture. Bark is pale grey and smooth. Tubular flowers have crinkly crimson petals; favoured by sunbirds. The **extraordinary fruits are up to 50 cm long**.

BIGNONIACEAE Height: up to 20 m

## *Jacaranda mimosifolia* \*
### Jacaranda

Handsome, deciduous tree with a broad crown. A **native of South America**, it is widely cultivated along streets and in parks and gardens, but **invades natural habitats**. Unmistakable when mauve blossom covers the tree in early summer. Leaves are compound, fern-like, yellow in winter. Fruits are flat woody capsules housing winged seeds.

BIGNONIACEAE Height: up to 20 m

## *Xanthocercis zambesiaca*
### Nyala Tree/Njalaboom

Impressive evergreen tree with broad dense crown. **Trunk is usually fluted with multiple coppice stems.** Grows along rivers but also on termite mounds. Giant specimen grows at Tshokwane in the KNP. Leaves compound with up to seven pairs of sub-opposite leaflets. Flowers inconspicuous. Small oval fruits yellowish when ripe; eaten by antelope.

FABACEAE Height: up to 30 m

## *Diospyros mespiliformis*
### Jackalberry/Jakkalsbessie

Impressive tree which reaches greatest size along watercourses, but also grows on termite mounds. Bark is dark, peeling off in square sections. **Simple leaves are alternate, oval and usually have wavy margins**. Flowers are tiny, pale yellow bells. Round berries ripen to yellow and are fed upon by birds, antelope, baboons and – it is said – by jackals. Loses leaves briefly at the end of winter.

EBENACEAE Height: up to 20 m

## Trichilia emetica
### Natal Mahogany/Rooiessenhout
Large **evergreen** tree with a dense rounded crown. Usually grows near water. Trunk is usually low-branching and covered in scaly bark. The compound leaves consist of up to eleven leaflets and a terminal one; dark green and glossy above, paler and hairy below. Small greenish flowers appear in spring. Spherical fruits split to reveal large, black and red seeds.
MELIACEAE Height: up to 20 m

## Ekebergia capensis
### Cape Ash/Essenhout
Large, semi-deciduous tree which may be evergreen in wetter conditions. Crown is dense with hanging foliage. Sparse in the KNP but grown in many restcamps; beautiful **coppery-red autumn foliage**. Small berries pale yellow, becoming red when ripe; loved by birds. Compound leaves with up to seven pairs of pointed leaflets, plus a terminal leaflet. Flowers are tiny.
MELIACEAE Height: up to 18 m

## Melia azederach *
### Syringa/Persian Lilac 🕱
Tall graceful tree with glossy, fern-like, compound leaves. A **native of south-east Asia**, it is a **vigorous invader**, particularly along streams so **should not be cultivated**. Small lilac flowers appear in dense clusters in spring, and are very fragrant. Yellow berries are produced in abundance in autumn – poisonous to man, but eaten by louries and other birds. Deciduous.
MELIACEAE Height: up to 20 m

## Spirostachys africana
### Tamboti/Tambotie 🕱
Medium-sized, deciduous tree which favours poorly drained soils along watercourses where it **often forms pure stands**. Stem is straight with **dark bark breaking up into small blocks**. Leaves small, alternate with scalloped margins; some turn scarlet in autumn. Flowers in spikes in spring. Fruit is a **three-lobed capsule**. Contains **poisonous white latex**.
EUPHORBIACEAE Height: up to 10 m

## *Sclerocarya birrea*
### Marula/Maroela

Large tree with a spreading crown. **Bark is pale grey, peeling off in disc-shaped flakes.** Leaves compound with 3 to 7 pairs of pointed leaflets, and a terminal leaflet, on long petioles. Flowers are tiny. Juicy **yellow fruits** ripen on the ground in mid-summer; relished by Elephant, Chacma Baboon and people. Deciduous; bare branches and stems point upwards.

ANACARDIACEAE Height: up to 15 m

## *Adansonia digitata*
### Baobab/Kremetartboom

Gigantic squat tree which may live for thousands of years. Unmistakable when leafless in winter. Bark is smooth and fibrous, and much favoured by Elephant. **Leaves are palmate** with five leaflets. Flowers are large and white, opening mostly at night and pollinated by bats. Seeds are in a dry white pulp in a large velvety pod. Only in northern Lowveld.

BOMBACACEAE Height: up to 25 m

## *Chorisia speciosa* *
### Brazilian Kapok

Large tree which resembles a Baobab but has a **greenish trunk covered in knobbly thorns**. Non-invasive ornamental **native to South America**; widely grown in towns. Puts on a magnificent display in autumn when **masses of pink flowers** cover the tree. Leaves palmate. Large oval fruits split to release seeds set in a woolly fleece (kapok).

BOMBACACEAE Height: up to 20 m

## *Breonadia salicina*
### Matumi/Mingerhout

Small to very large upright tree which grows along rivers and streams. May form a pointed pyramid shape. Stem is grey-brown with ridged bark. Leaves simple, oblong and very glossy. Small **flowers packed in ball-shaped** heads. The similar *Rauvolfia caffra* – Quinine Tree – also grows along rivers but has drooping foliage and fawn-coloured bark.

RUBIACEAE Height: up to 20 m

### *Combretum imberbe*
**Leadwood/Hardekool**

Large deciduous tree with a straight trunk and sparse crown. Leaves are small, grey-green, in opposite pairs; young stems spine tipped. Bark is grey, with **texture of elephant skin**. Small, **four-winged fruits are pale yellow**. The wood is hard and heavy. May live for thousands of years; dead specimens remain standing for ages. Favours poorly-drained soils.
COMBRETACEAE Height: up to 20 m

### *Combretum hereroense*
**Russet Bushwillow/Kierieklapper**

Small deciduous tree with crooked branches often trailing close to the ground. Leaves are small, dark green above and paler below; in opposite pairs. Bark is variable, fissured in older trees. Small, four-winged **fruits are rusty-red** and cover the entire tree in summer. Flowers inconspicuous. Often grows in association with Mopane on clay soils.
COMBRETACEAE Height: up to 8 m

### *Combretum apiculatum*
**Red Bushwillow/Rooiboswilg**

Small deciduous tree with crooked branches and spare crown; often multi-stemmed. Leaves are broad with **tips pointed and twisted**; in opposite pairs. Yellow-cream flowers are in spikes in spring with new foliage. Bark is greyish, cracking into small flakes. Small, four-winged fruits are reddish-green, drying to brown. Often **abundant on dry slopes**.
COMBRETACEAE Height: up to 9 m

### *Combretum microphyllum*
**Flame Creeper/Vlamklimop**

Twining climber which reaches into tall trees along watercourses. Inconspicuous for much of the year but spectacular in September to October, when **stems massed with clusters of tiny scarlet flowers**. The pale, four-winged fruits which follow become brown. Stems armed with spines. Leaves opposite or sub-opposite. Semi-deciduous.
COMBRETACEAE Height: up to 10 m

## *Terminalia sericea*
### Silver Terminalia/Vaalboom

Tall graceful tree with distinctive, **silvery-green foliage**. Typically grows in deep sands, or above 'seep-lines' where clay and sandy soils meet. Bark is dark and deeply furrowed. Leaves are borne in clusters. Flowers are in spikes and have a **pungent scent**. Fruits are pinkish-grey. Branchlets are often covered in swollen galls caused by larvae of small insects.

COMBRETACEAE Height: up to 20 m

## *Terminalia prunioides*
### Purplepod Terminalia/Sterkbos

Dense tangled shrub or small tree which usually grows in shallow, poorly drained soils. The small, dark green leaves have a squared-off tip; in clusters. The bark is grey and furrowed, and the wood heavy and hard. White flowers are borne in dense spikes in summer. **Reddish-purple fruits** may cover the tree throughout the winter. Deciduous.

COMBRETACEAE Height: up to 8 m

## *Dombeya rotundifolia*
### Common Wild Pear/Drolpeer

Crooked bushy tree typical of hillsides, and most conspicuous in August when it is covered in masses of **papery white flowers**, which fade to russet-brown. Bark is dark and furrowed. Roundish leaves are alternate, irregularly toothed and coarsely textured. Fruits are inconspicuous capsules. Fire-resistant and hardy. Deciduous.

STERCULIACEAE Height: up to 8 m

## *Sterculia murex*
### Lowveld Chestnut/Laeveldkastaiing

Medium-sized tree with crooked stem and open branches; bark is grey and grooved. Restricted to hilly country around Nelspruit, Barberton and Pretoriuskop. Palmate leaves have 5 to 9 oblong leaflets; become yellow and rust-red in autumn. Leafless tree bears clusters of **yellow, waxy flowers** from early August to September. Edible black seeds are housed in a large **spiny capsule** which ripens in midsummer.

STERCULIACEAE Height: up to 10 m

111

## *Euphorbia ingens*
### Tree Euphorbia/Naboom
Medium-sized, cactus-like tree with a dense crown of succulent, **4-angled branches in oblong sections**. Leafless; exudes poisonous latex. Widespread.

EUPHORBIACEAE  Height: up to 15 m

## *Euphorbia cooperi*
### Candelabra Tree/Kandelaarnaboom
Small, cactus-like tree with outstretched crown of succulent, **5-angled branches in heart-shaped sections**. Leafless; exudes poisonous latex. Grows among rocks.

EUPHORBIACEAE  Height: up to 5 m

## *Cussonia spicata*
### Common Cabbage Tree/Kiepersol
Slender evergreen tree with **bushy crown of palmate leaves**; single or multi-stemmed. Flowers in candelabra spike. Rare in KNP, but common in escarpment foothills.

ARALIACEAE  Height: up to 8 m (20 m in forest)

## *Commiphora marlothii*
### Paperbark Corkwood/Kanniedood
Crooked deciduous tree with distinctive **green bark** which peels off in papery yellow sheets. Leaves compound, hairy. Grows only on rocky outcrops.

BURSERACEAE  Height: up to 8 m

## *Gardenia volkensii*
### Savanna Gardenia/Katjiepiering
Small thickset tree with angular stems. Leaves leathery; borne in threes at stem tips. **Flowers open white but turn yellow within days**. Fruit is a ribbed drupe.

RUBIACEAE  Height: up to 8 m

## *Euclea divinorum*
### Magic Guarri/Towerghwarrie
Dense evergreen shrub typical of poorly drained soils. Slender **leaves are shiny with wavy margins**. Frayed twig ends can be used as a toothbrush. Flowers tiny.

EBENACEAE  Height: up to 5 m

## *Syzygium cordatum*
### Waterberry/Waterbessie
Medium-sized, **evergreen** tree, usually grows near water. Leaves oval, waxy; opposite; **petioles very short or absent.** Flowers white. Ripe berries purple-black.
MYRTACEAE Height: up to 15 m

## *Heteropyxis natalensis*
### Lavender Tree/Laventelboom
Medium-sized, deciduous tree with drooping foliage. **Bark fawn to white**; darker sections peel off. **Leaves strongly scented.** Common in hills west of KNP.
HETEROPYXIDACEAE Height: up to 8 m

## *Eucalyptus grandis* *
### Saligna Gum
Large tree **native to Australia** but grown in plantations in escarpment foothills; **invades disturbed soils.** Leaves lance-shaped; bark peels off in strips.
MYRTACEAE Height: up to 30 m

## *Pinus patula* *
### Patula Pine
Large coniferous tree **native to central America** but grown in plantations in escarpment foothills; **invades grasslands. Needles hang down in clusters.**
PINACEAE Height: up to 15 m

## *Kirkia accuminata*
### White Syringa/Witsering
Medium-sized, deciduous tree restricted to rocky outcrops. Compound leaves have 6 to 10 pairs of lance-shaped leaflets; foliage turns **coppery-red in autumn.**
SIMAROUBACEAE Height: up to 15 m

## *Strychnos madagascariensis*
### Black Monkeyorange/Swartklapper
Small, spineless, crooked tree with dense crown. **Leaves brittle with five bold veins** – three originating at the base. Large **fruits blue-green, orange when ripe.**
LOGANIACEAE Height: up to 8 m

## Lantana camara *
### Lantana
Shrub or climber with **prickly stems**.
Flower heads distinctively two-toned –
pink or yellow. Berries eaten by birds.
**Invasive alien** native to Central America.
VERBENACEAE Height: up to 4 m

## Caesalpinia decapetala *
### Mauritius Thorn
Scrambling shrub with **acacia-like leaves**
and **hooked thorns**. Flat pods with small
'beak'. Yellow flowers held in erect spike.
**Invasive alien** native to Central America.
CAESALPINIACEAE Height: up to 5 m

## Sesbania punicea *
### Brazilian Glory Pea
Multi-stemmed shrub with drooping
branches. Flowers **orange, pea-shaped**;
pods 4-angled. **Invasive alien** from
South America. Occurs along streams.
FABACEAE Height: up to 3 m

## Tecoma stans *
### Yellow Bells
Shrub or small tree with compound
leaves; semi-deciduous. **Golden-yellow,
bell-shaped flowers**; pods long, papery.
**Invasive alien** from Tropical America.
BIGNONIACEAE Height: up to 4 m

## Solanum mauritianum *
### Bugweed Tree
Shrub or small tree with slender branches.
Leaves oval, pointed, hairy; foul smelling.
Flowers lilac, star-shaped. Berries eaten by
birds. **Invasive alien** from Trop. America.
SOLANACEAE Height: up to 3 m

## Psidium guajava *
### Guava
Shrub or small tree with patterned,
satin-like bark. Leaves oval with bold
veining. Fruit is a drupe with bracts at tip.
**Invasive alien** from Tropical America.
MYRTACEAE Height: up to 3 m

## *Phyllanthus reticulatus*
### Potatobush/Aartappelbos
Multi-stemmed shrub or climber with small, oval, alternate leaves. Small greenish flowers have **rich baked potato smell**; most obvious along rivers in evenings.
EUPHORBIACEAE Height: up to 4 m

## *Grewia monticola*
### Silver Raisin/Vaalrosyntjie
Small deciduous tree or tangled shrub. Leaves alternate, mid-green, **pale grey or white below**; asymmetrical at base. Yellow star flowers; berries 1- or 2-lobed.
TILIACEAE Height: up to 5 m

## *Tetradenia riparia*
### Wild Ginger/Wildesalie
Multi-stemmed, aromatic shrub with **hairy, heart-shaped leaves. Lilac or white flowers** in winter. Associated with granite outcrops; good garden subject.
LAMIACEAE Height: up to 2 m

## *Tecomaria capensis*
### Cape Honeysuckle/Kanferfoelie
Evergreen shrub or climber with compound leaves. **Trumpet-shaped flowers orange or yellow**; pods papery. Widely cultivated in gardens and KNP restcamps.
BIGNONIACEAE Height: up to 3 m

## *Dalbergia armata*
### Thorny Rope/Doringtou
Tangled climber or dense impenetrable shrub with **fierce spines on stems**. Leaves acacia-like, feathery. Flowers white, pea-shaped. Pods thin, reddish.
FABACEAE Height: 2 m or more

## *Clematis brachiata*
### Traveller's Joy/Klimop
Twining climber which sprawls over trees, shrubs and fences. Delicate white flowers appear in abundance in autumn, .followed by fluffy seeds.
RANUNCULACEAE Height: 2 m or more

# Succulents and Soft-stemmed Plants

In this section, only a small selection of the more noticeable plants are featured. There is great variety of small herbs and succulents in the area, with the majority being rather difficult for the beginner to identify. In a few instances, the species depicted here may be uncommon in their natural habitat but have been included as they are widely cultivated in KNP restcamps or in gardens around hotels and lodges, and are therefore frequently seen by casual visitors.

Two of the aloes below, as well as some of the plants opposite, could easily be classified as shrubs but are featured in this section to allow comparison with their smaller relatives.

The identification of smaller plants may be a complex matter with subtle differences separating members of the same family. The best regional guide to the smaller flowering plants is *A Field Guide to Wild Flowers of KwaZulu-Natal and the Eastern Region* by Elsa Pooley (Natal Flora, Durban), which describes and illustrates the great majority of species in the Kruger and along the escarpment.

### *Aloe marlothii*
**Mountain Aloe/Bergaalwyn**

Tall, single-stemmed tree aloe with fleshy, blue-grey leaves, armed with small spines. Stem covered in dry leaves. Orange flowers on branched 'arms' from June to August.

Asphodelaceae Height: up to 3 m

### *Aloe spicata* (= A. sessiliflora)
**Lebombo Aloe/Lebombo-aalwyn**

Short-stemmed aloe with narrow, strap-like leaves; pale green or brick-red in full sun. Yellow flowers are in erect spikes in winter. Grows on cliffs and rocks.

Asphodelaceae

JOHN BURROWS

### *Aloe chabaudii*
**Cluster Aloe/Blougroen-aalwyn**

Small stemless aloe with slender, blue-green leaves. Grows in clusters on flat ground or at the base of rocks. **Open spikes of orange flowers** in midwinter.

Asphodelaceae

### *Aloe petricola*
**Rock Aloe/Rotsaalwyn**

Small stemless aloe with thick, blue-green leaves. Grows on granite outcrops south of the Sabie River. **Dense spikes of red and cream** flowers appear in midwinter.

Asphodelaceae

## Adenium multiflorum
### Impala Lily/Impalalelie
Stocky shrub with thick succulent stems.
Leaves are waxy and glossy green. Star-
shaped pink and white flowers appear in
winter; many planted in KNP restcamps.

APOCYNACEAE  Height: up to 2 m

## Pachypodium saundersii
### Kudu Lily/Koedoelelie
Succulent shrub of rocky outcrops with
swollen stem and trailing branches armed
with spines. Leaves glossy green with
wavy margins. White flowers in autumn.

APOCYNACEAE  Height: up to 2 m

## Ricinus communis *
### Castoroil Bush
Small shrub with waxy stems and large,
**star-shaped leaves**. **Invasive alien** from
N.E. Africa which grows along roads and
streams. Spiny fruits in an erect spike.

EUPHORBIACEAE  Height: up to 2 m

## Opuntia ficus-indica *
### Sweet Prickly Pear
Succulent shrub or small tree with **paddle-
shaped stems** armed with spines; leafless.
Fruits plum-shaped, spiny and edible.
**Invasive alien** from Central America.

CACTACEAE  Height: up to 2 m

## Crinum macowanii
### River Crinum/Rivierlelie
Robust lily with dark green, strap-like
leaves with **wavy margins**. Snow white
or pale pink, bell-shaped flowers appear
in early summer; buds are striped pink.

AMARYLLIDACEAE

## Cleome angustifolia
### Golden Cleome/Wildebosganna
Delicate, open-branched herb with thin
compound leaves. Yellow flowers have
purple base and distinctive protruding
stamens. Common along roadsides.

CAPPARACEAE

## *Gloriosa superba* 🏵️
### Flame Lily/Vlamlelie
Climbing herb which sprawls over rocks
or low bushes. Glossy leaves have twining
tips. **Yellow flowers have flame-like
petals and outstretched stamens.**
LILIACEAE   Height: up to 1 m

## *Ansellia gigantea*
### Leopard Orchid/Luiperdorgidee
Epiphytic orchid with roots anchored on
the branch of a tree, often in full sunlight.
Fragrant yellow flowers sometimes
spotted brown, in August to September.
ORCHIDACEAE

## *Hibiscus engleri*
### Wild Hibiscus/Wildehibiskus
One of several yellow-flowered hibiscus
typified by **5 large petals and branched
style.** Pink species also common. Some
are invasive weeds from other countries.
MALVACEAE   Height: up to 2.5 m

## *Leonotis ocymifolia*
### Wild Dagga/Wildedagga
Sparse shrub with tall, 4-angled stems
with **spiky, golfball-sized heads** spaced
up the stems supporting **tubular orange
flowers.** Sunbirds feed on the nectar.
LAMIACEAE   Height: up to 2.5 m

## *Jasminum stenolobum*
### Rock Jasmine
Scrambler with lance-shaped leaves;
favours exposed rocky sites. **Fragrant,
star-shaped flowers** are white; pink
below. Green berries ripen to black.
OLEACEAE

## *Vernonia colorata*
### River Vernonia
Bushy shrub common along watercourses
and roadsides. Broad oval leaves with
wavy margins. **Fluffy, pale lilac flowers
in dense terminal clusters** in autumn.
ASTERACEAE   Height: up to 2 m

## *Dicerocaryum zanguebarium*
### Devil's Thorn/Beesdubbeltjie
Small annual herb with **trailing stems**.
Leaves opposite, toothed. Flowers pink-
mauve, trumpet-shaped. Seeds held in
**flattish capsule with 2 erect spines**.
PEDALIACEAE

## *Ceratotheca triloba*
### Wild Foxglove/Vingerhoedblom
Tall annual herb with **erect stems**. Leaves
opposite, 3-lobed, toothed. Flowers pale
pink or white, **elongate, trumpet-shaped**.
Occurs among rocks or along roadsides.
PEDIALACEAE   Height: up to 2.5 m

## *Nymphaea nouchali*
### Day Waterlily/Waterlelie
Aquatic plant with round, floating leaves
split by a V-notch. **Flowers may be white,
blue or pink**; open by day. Occurs in pans,
dams and pools in slow-flowing rivers.
NYMPHAEACEAE

## *Eichhornia crassipes* *
### Water Hyacinth
Aquatic plant with fleshy green leaves
and **swollen petiole**. Flowers are mauve.
Rampant **invasive alien** from Tropical
America which **smothers water surfaces**.
PONTEDERIACEAE

## *Abrus precatorius* ☠
### Luckybean Creeper
Twining vine with pinnate leaves. Small,
mauve, pea-shaped flowers are in clusters.
Pods are distinctive triangular capsules
holding **scarlet 'lucky-bean' seeds**.
FABACEAE

## *Gerbera jamesonii*
### Barberton Daisy/Madeliefie
Small daisy with a rosette of **irregularly
shaped leaves**; often deeply divided.
Flowers may be red, pink, orange or
yellow; appear from August to December.
ASTERACEAE

# Grasses

Grasses play a vital role in the ecology of ecosystems, particularly in African savannas where they support large numbers of grazing herbivores. By way of an introduction to this difficult-to-identify family, a few of the more common and distinctive species are described here. Grass flowers are in **spikes**, which are borne on single **culms** (stems) or on branched **panicles**.

For more information, *The Guide to Grasses of Southern Africa* by Frits van Oudtshoorn and Eben van Wyk (Briza, 1999) is recommended.

## *Phragmites australis*
### Common Reed
Tall aquatic grass with densely packed, white or pale spikes. Leaf blades are strap-like and razor sharp. Abundant in riverbeds and around dams. Perennial.
POACEAE  Height: up to 4 m

## *Cenchrus ciliaris*
### Blue Buffalo Grass/Bloubuffelgras
**Tufted perennial** with 8 mm leaf blades. Inflorescence a **dense cylindrical spike**. Palatable grass favoured by Buffalo and other grazing herbivores.
POACEAE  Height: up to 1 m

## *Panicum maximum*
### Guinea Grass/Gewone Buffelsgras
**Tufted perennial** with 30 mm leaf blades. Inflorescence an **open panicle**. Highly palatable, favoured by all grazing herbivores; grows tallest in shade.
POACEAE  Height: up to 2.5 m

## *Digitaria eriantha*
### Finger Grass/Vingergras
**Tufted perennial** with 14 mm leaf blades. Inflorescence with **3 to 15 spikes** in one or two whorls at the culm tip. Palatable; often grows near water.
POACEAE  Height: up to 1 m

## *Perotis patens*
### Cat's Tail Grass/Katstertgras
**Tufted annual** with 12 mm leaf blades. Inflorescence an attractive **soft, straight spike**. Occurs in disturbed soils, often in dry, exposed sites. Unpalatable.
POACEAE  Height: up to 60 cm

## *Hyperthelia dissoluta*
### Yellow Thatching Grass
Tall **tufted perennial** with 12 mm leaf blades. Inflorescence purplish-red with yellow awns. Popular thatching grass. Often abundant along roadsides.
POACEAE Height: up to 3 m

## *Heteropogon contortus*
### Spear Grass/Assegaaigras
**Tufted perennial** with 7 mm leaf blades. Inflorescence a terminal spike with **long awns which become entangled** and may pierce skin. Often common along roads.
POACEAE Height: up to 2.5 m

## *Themeda triandra*
### Red Grass/Rooigras
**Tufted perennial** with 8 mm leaf blades. Inflorescence a false panicle of drooping, V-shaped spikes. Palatable in summer; turns red and brittle in winter.
POACEAE Height: up to 1.5 m

FRITS VAN OUDTSHOORN

## *Cymbopogon plurinodes*
### Narrow Turpentine Grass
**Tufted perennial** with 4 mm leaf blades. Inflorescence a false panicle of up to eight paired spikes. **Strong turpentine smell** and taste. Unpalatable except when young.
POACEAE Height: up to 1 m

## *Dactyloctenium australe*
### L.M. Grass/L.M.-gras
**Creeping perennial** grass which thrives in shade and is the most **popular lawn grass** in Lowveld gardens. Inflorescence with 2 or 3 spikes at tip. Nutritious.
POACEAE Height: 20 cm

## *Melinis repens*
### Redtop Grass/Rooipluimgras
**Tufted annual** with 11 mm leaf blades. Inflorescence an open panicle; **spikelets with red or pink hairs** which age to white. Abundant along roadsides.
POACEAE Height: up to 1 m

# REFERENCES AND FURTHER READING

## GEOLOGY

Pritchard, J.M. 1986. *Landscape and Landform in Africa*. Edward Arnold, London.

Schutte, I.C. 1986. 'The General Geology of the Kruger National Park'. *Koedoe* 29: 13-37. National Parks Board of S.A., Pretoria.

Viljoen, M.J. & Reimold, W.U. 1999. *An Introduction to South Africa's Geological and Mining Heritage*. Mintek, Johannesburg.

## MAMMALS

Apps, P. & du Toit, R. 2000. *Creatures of Habit: Understanding African Animal Behaviour*. Struik, Cape Town.

Estes, R.D. 1995. *Behaviour Guide to African Mammals*. Russel Friedman Books, Halfway House.

Kingdon, J. 1997. *The Kingdon Field Guide to African Mammals*. Academic Press, London.

Pienaar, U. de V., Rautenbach, I.L. & De Graaf, G. 1980. *The Small Mammals of the Kruger National Park*. National Parks Board, Pretoria.

Skinner, J.D. & Smithers, R.H.N. 1990. *The Mammals of the Southern African Subregion* (2nd edition). University of Pretoria, Pretoria.

Stuart, C. & T. 1997. *Field Guide to the Larger Mammals of Southern Africa*. Struik, Cape Town.

## BIRDS

Gibbon, G. 1991. *Southern African Bird Sounds* (set of 6 cassettes). SA Birding cc, Durban.

Ginn, P.J., McIlleron, W.G. & Milstein, P. le S. 1989. *The Complete Book of Southern African Birds*. Struik Winchester, Cape Town.

Hall, D.G. 1983. *Birds of Mataffin, Eastern Transvaal*. Southern Birds 10: Witwatersrand Bird Club, Johannesburg.

MacLean, G.L. (Ed.) 1993. *Roberts' Birds of Southern Africa* (6th edition). John Voelcker Bird Book Fund, Cape Town.

Newman, K. 1989. *Birds of the Kruger National Park*. Southern Books, Halfway House.

Sinclair, I., Hayman, P. & Arlott, N. 1993. *Sasol Birds of Southern Africa*. Struik, Cape Town.

Sinclair, I. & Whyte. I. 1992. *Birds of the Kruger National Park*. Struik, Cape Town.

Steyn, P. 1996. *Nesting Birds: The Breeding Habits of Southern African Birds*. Fernwood, Cape Town.

Tarboten, W. & Erasmus, R. 1998. *Owls and Owling in Southern Africa*. Struik, Cape Town.

Van Perlo, B. 1999. *Birds of Southern Africa: Collins Illustrated Checklist*. Harper Collins, London

## REPTILES

Branch, B. 1988. *Field Guide to the Snakes and Other Reptiles of Southern Africa*. Struik, Cape Town.

Broadley, D.G. 1983. *Fitzsimons' Snakes of Southern Africa*. Delta Books, Johannesburg.

Pienaar, U de V., Haacke, W.D. & Jacobsen, N.H.G. 1978. *The Reptiles of the Kruger National Park*. National Parks Board of S.A., Pretoria.

## FROGS

Passmore, N.I. & Carruthers, V.C. 1995. *South African Frogs* (2nd edition). Southern Books, Halfway House &Wits Univ. Press, Johannesburg.

Pienaar, U. de V., Passmore, N.I. & Carruthers,V.C. 1976. *The Frogs of the Kruger National Park*. National Parks Board of S.A., Pretoria.

## FRESHWATER FISHES

Pienaar, U. de V. 1968. *The Freshwater Fishes of the Kruger National Park*. National Parks Board of S.A. Pretoria.

Skelton, P.H. 1993. *A Complete Guide to the Freshwater Fishes of Southern Africa*. Southern Books, Halfway House.

## INVERTEBRATES

Braack, L.E.O. 1991. *Field Guide to Insects of the Kruger National Park*. Struik, Cape Town.

Leroy, A. & J. *Spiderwatch in Southern Africa*. Struik, Cape Town.

Pinhey, E.C.G. 1975. *Moths of Southern Africa*. Tafelberg, Cape Town.

Pringle, E.L.L., Henning, G.A. & Ball, J.B. (Eds.) 1994. *Pennington's Butterflies of Southern Africa* (2nd edition). Struik, Cape Town.

Skaife, S.H. (revised by J.A. Ledger). 1979. *African Insect Life*. Struik, Cape Town.

Weaving, A. 2000. *Southern African Insects and their World*. Struik, Cape Town.

Williams, M. 1994. *Butterflies of Southern Africa: A Field Guide*. Southern Books, Halfway House.

## PLANTS

Coates Palgrave, K. 1983. *Trees of Southern Africa*. Struik, Cape Town.

Pooley, E. 1998. *A Field Guide to the Wild Flowers of KwaZulu-Natal and the Eastern Region*. Natal Flora, Durban.

Scholes, R.J. 1986. *A Guide to Bush Clearing in the Eastern Transvaal Lowveld*. Resource Ecology Group, Univ. of Wits, Johannesburg.

Van Oudtshoorn, F. & Van Wyk, E. 1999. *Guide to Grasses of Southern Africa*. Briza, Pretoria.

Van Wyk, P. 1984. *Field Guide to the Trees of the Kruger National Park*. Struik, Cape Town.

## PICTORIAL

Voigt, L. 1999. *Lulu Phezulu – a miscellany of Paintings, Curiosities, Lore and Legend by a Bushveld Naturalist*. David Philip, Cape Town.

## HISTORY

Carruthers, J. 1995. *The Kruger National Park: A Social and Political History*. University of Natal Press, Pietermaritzburg.

Stevenson-Hamilton, J. 1934. *The Lowveld: Its Wildlife and its People*. Cassell, London.

Stevenson-Hamilton, J. 1937. *South African Eden*. Cassell, London (and 1993, Struik, Cape Town).

# USEFUL CONTACT ADDRESSES

**LOWVELD INFO**
*Information and reservations
for wildlife reserves (including
Kruger National Park restcamps) outdoor activities and
accommodation. Also information and contact details of
local tour and nature guides.*
PO Box 5018, Nelspruit, 1200
Tel. (013) 755 1988
www.lowveldinfo.com

**KRUGER NATIONAL PARK**
*Reservations for Pretoriuskop,
Berg en Dal, Skukuza, Lower
Sabie, Satara, Letaba,
Shingwedzi, Olifants, Punda
Maria and other restcamps.*
Tel. Nelspruit: (013) 752 1988
or (013) 752 4547
Skukuza (013) 735 4060
Pretoria (012) 343 1991
Skukuza Research
Management (013) 735 4000
www.parks-sa.co.za

**MPUMALANGA PARKS
BOARD**
*Nature conservation agency
and reservations for lodgings
at Blyde River Canyon,
Songimvelo and Mahushe-
Shongwe wildlife reserves.*

PO Box 1990, Nelspruit 1200
Tel. (013) 759 5432
or (013) 752 7001
www.mpumalanga.com

**NORTHERN PROVINCE
ENVIRONMENTAL
AFFAIRS AND TOURISM**
*Nature conservation agency
and information on protected
areas including Manyeleti,
Andover, Makuya and
Nwanedi wildlife reserves.*
PO Box 217, Pietersberg 0070
Tel. (015) 295 9300

**C.C. AFRICA**
*Reservations for Londolozi,
Ngala and Bongani private
game lodges.*
P/Bag X11, Benmore 2010
Tel. (011) 809 4300
www.ccafrica.com

**SWAZILAND TRUST
COMMISION**
*Reservations for accommoda-
tion at Mlawula, Hlane and
Malalotja wildlife reserves.*
PO Box 234, Mbabane, Swaziland
Tel. (09268) 4161151

**BIRDLIFE LOWVELD**
*Formerly known as Lowveld*

*Bird Club. Active group which
undertakes outings and organ-
ises evening meetings.
Produces an informative quar-
terly bulletin – 'The Hornbill'.*
PO Box 19334, Nelspruit, 1200
www.birdlife.org.sa

**PLANT SPECIALIST
GROUP**
*Small but active group, open
to new members, which
explores botanical interests in
the Lowveld and Escarpment
regions. Monthly meetings and
occasional outings.*
PO Box 710, Lyndenburg 1120

**BOTANICAL SOCIETY
(LOWVELD BRANCH)**
*Local branch of national
organisation. Regular outings
and guest speakers.*
PO Box 974, Nelspruit 1200

**LOWVELD BOTANICAL
GARDEN**
*Marvelous gardens with vast
collection of African plants in
semi-formal and semi-wild
landscapes. Excellent nursery
of indigenous trees and shrubs.*
PO Box 1024, Nelspruit 1200
Tel. (013) 752 5531

# GLOSSARY OF SCIENTIFIC TERMS

**alien** – an organism introduced by man, and now naturalised in a region or country in which it does not belong
**alluvial** – deposit of soil or sand left by flood
**alternate** – leaves which are arranged singly at different points on a stem
**anal** – rear end, anus
**anther** – pollen-bearing part of a flower
**aquatic** – living in water
**arboreal** – living in trees
**awn** – bristle-like extension to bracts surrounding inflorescence of grasses
**axil** – upper joint between a leaf and a stem
**bipinnate** – a compound leaf in which the leaflets are further divided into pinna (eg *Acacia*)
**bract** – leaf-like structure from which a flower arises
**calcrete** – white laterite rock rich in calcium
**compound** – a leaf consisting of several leaflets (eg *Kigelia*)
**crepuscular** – active at twilight, or just before dawn

**deciduous** – a plant which sheds its leaves at the end of the growing season
**dorsal** – upper surface of the body
**dorsal fin** – fin on the spine of a fish
**drupe** – a fleshy, non-splitting fruit
**epiphyte** – an organism that grows on another but is not parasitic
**gills** – breathing organs of fishes
**herbivorous** – eating plant matter
**indigenous** – an organism occur-ring naturally in an area
**latex** – a white, sticky liquid
**leaflet** – divided leaf
**mimic** – one animal resembling the form or colour of another, in order to obtain some benefit
**native** – *see* indigenous
**naturalised** – an organism which has been introduced from elsewhere and is reproducing successfully in a new area
**opposite** – leaves which are arranged opposite to one another on a stem
**panicle** – branched inflorescence
**parasite** – an organism which obtains its food from another organism (host)

**perennial plant** – a plant which lives for at least three years
**perennial river** – a river which flows throughout the year
**petiole** – leaf stalk
**pinna** – divided part of a leaflet
**pinnate** – a compound leaf divided into leaflets
**roost** – nighttime resting place of birds or bats
**serrated** – margin notched with fine projections
**simple leaf** – an undivided leaf
**scale** – a thin, plate-like structure
**scalloped** – leaf margin notched with blunt projections
**spike** – an elongated stem which bears more than one flower
**terminal** – at the end of a stem
**terrestrial** – living on the ground
**toothed** – leaf margin notched with pointed projections
**trifoliate** – a leaf which is divided into three leaflets
**ventral** – undersurface
**whorled** – the arrangement of three or more leaves or flowers at the same point on a stem to form an encircling ring

# INDEX OF FEATURED SPECIES

125

*Ekebergia capensis* 108
*Erythrina lysistemon* 106
*Eucalyptus grandis* * 113
*Euclea divinorum* 112
*Euphorbia cooperi* 112
*Euphorbia ingens* 112
*Faidherbia albida* 103
Fever Tree 103
*Ficus abutilifolia* 101
*Ficus glumosa* 101
*Ficus sycomorous* 101
*Ficus thonningii* 101
Fig, Largeleaved Rock 101
Fig, Mountain 101
Fig, Strangler 101
Fig, Sycamore 101
Flamboyant * 106
Flame Thorn 103
Flame Creeper 110
Flame Lily 118
Flame Tree, African * 106
Foxglove, Wild 119
Gardenia, Savanna 112
*Gardenia volkensii* 112
*Gerbera jamesonii* 119
*Gloriosa superba* 118
*Grewia monticola* 115
Guarri, Magic 112
Guava * 114
Gum, Saligna * 113
*Heteropyxis natalensis* 113
*Hibiscus engleri* 118
Hibiscus, Wild 118
Honeysuckle, Cape 115
*Hyphaene coriacea* 100
Impala Lily 117
Jacaranda * 107
*Jacaranda mimosifolia* * 107
Jackalberry 107
Jasmine, Rock 118
*Jasminum stenolobum* 118
Kapok, Brazilian * 109
Kiaat 105
*Kigelia africana* 107
*Kirkia accuminata* 113
Knob Thorn 102
Kudu Lily 117
Lala Palm 100
Lantana * 114
*Lantana camara* * 114

Leadwood 110
*Leonotis ocymifolia* 118
*Lonchocarpus capassa* 105
Luckybean Creeper 119
Mahogany, Pod 104
Mahogany, Natal 108
Marula 109
Matumi 109
Mauritius Thorn * 114
Monkeyorange, Black 113
*Melia azederach* * 108
Mopane 104
Nyala Tree 107
*Nymphaea nouchali* 119
*Opuntia ficus-indica* * 117
Orchid, Leopard 118
*Pachypodium saundersii* 117
Palm, Lala 100
Palm, Wild Date 100
Paperbark Thorn 102
*Peltophorum africanum* 105
Persian Lilac * 108
*Phoenix reclinata* 100
*Phyllanthus reticulatus* 115
Pine, Patula * 113
*Pinus patula* * 113
Potatobush 115
Prickly Pear, Sweet * 117
Pride-of-De-Kaap 106
*Psidium guajava* *. 114
*Pterocarpus angolensis* 105
Rain Tree 105
Raisin, Silver 115
*Ricinus communis* * 117
Sausage Tree 107
Scented Thorn 102
*Schotia brachypetela* 104
*Sclerocarya birrea* 109
*Sesbania punicea* * 114
Sicklebush 103
*Solanum mauritianum* * 114
*Spathodea campanulata* * 106
*Spirostachys africana* 108
*Sterculia murex* 111
*Strychnos madagascariensis* 113
Syringa * 108
Syringa, White 113
*Syzygium cordatum* 113
Tamboti 108
*Tecoma stans* * 114

*Tecomaria capensis* 115
*Terminalia pruniodes* 111
Terminalia, Purplepod 111
*Terminalia sericea* 111
Terminalia, Silver 111
*Tetradenia riparia* 115
Thorny Rope 115
Traveller's Joy 115
Tree Euphorbia 112
Tree Wisteria 104
*Trichelia emetica* 108
Umbrella Thorn 102
*Vernonia colorata* 118
Vernonia, River 118
Waterberry 113
Water Hyacinth * 119
Waterlily, Day 119
Wattle, Weeping 105
Weeping Boerbean 104
Wild Dagga 118
Wild Date Palm 100
Wild Ginger 115
Wild Pear, Common 111
*Xanthocercis zambesiaca* 107
Yellow Bells * 114

## GRASSES

Buffalo Grass, Blue 120
Cat's Tail Grass 120
*Cenchrus ciliaris* 120
*Cymbopogon plurinodes* 121
*Dactyloctenium australe* 121
*Digitaria eriantha* 120
Finger Grass 120
Guinea Grass 120
*Heteropogon contortus* 121
*Hyperthelia dissoluta* 121
L.M. Grass 121
*Melinis repens* 121
*Panicum maximum* 120
*Perotis patens* 120
*Phragmites australis* 120
Reed, Common 120
Red Grass 121
Redtop Grass 121
Spear Grass 121
Thatching Grass, Yellow 121
*Themeda triandra* 121
Turpentine Grass, Narrow 121